Christian Social Union

Abreast of the Times

A course of sermons on social subjects organized by the London Branch of the Christian Social Union, and preached in the Church of St. Edmund, King and Martyr, Lombard Street, during Lent, 1894.

Christian Social Union

Abreast of the Times
A course of sermons on social subjects organized by the London Branch of the Christian Social Union, and preached in the Church of St. Edmund, King and Martyr, Lombard Street, during Lent, 1894.

ISBN/EAN: 9783337264659

Printed in Europe, USA, Canada, Australia, Japan

Cover: Foto ©Lupo / pixelio.de

More available books at **www.hansebooks.com**

ABREAST OF THE

A COURSE OF

Sermons on Social Subjects

*...NIZED BY THE LONDON BRANCH OF THE CHRISTIAN
...CIAL UNION, AND PREACHED IN THE CHURCH OF
ST. EDMUND, KING AND MARTYR, LOMBARD
STREET, DURING LENT, 1894.*

With a Preface
BY
THE BISHOP OF DURHAM.

NEW YORK:
...S POTT & CO., 114 FIFTH AVENUE.
1894.

NOTE.

THESE Sermons were preached, by kind permission of the Rector, Canon Benham, in the Church of St. Edmund, King and Martyr, Lombard Street, E.C., during Lent, 1894. The series was organized by the London Branch of the Christian Social Union. The idea of the promoters was to bring vividly before the minds of business men and others that the pressing Social Problems of the day would be the fittest object of their thoughts, prayers, heart-searchings, and aspirations during the solemn season of Lent; and that, as Christians, they were bound to seek for direction in their solution from their Lord and Master Jesus Christ.

For the benefit of those who may desire to know, the objects of the Christian Social Union are printed elsewhere.

H S. HOLLAND,
Chairman of Committee.

PREFACE.

THE course of sermons contained in this volume was organized by the London branch of the Christian Social Union, but each preacher was left perfectly free to speak according to his mind, and is alone responsible for his own sermon.

I have not had the advantage of hearing or reading any of the sermons, but the striking variety of subjects and writers illustrates the wide field which the Union occupies and the liberty which is allowed to the members — though I believe that the writers are not all members of the Union — in regard to their economic and political and theological opinions. At the same time, I cannot doubt that whatever differences may exist in the methods and the conclusions of the several contributors, all alike recognise the same motive and the same principle and the same power of Christian action; the motive and the principle and the power which are to be found in the application of the fact of the Incarnation to the manifold problems of life in dependence on the Holy Spirit sent in the name of Jesus Christ.

The popular misconception of the scope and

strength of Christianity, which must be due, in part at least, to the fault of believers, lays upon every Christian the duty of making clear to himself and to others what he holds the faith to be as a social no less than an individual Gospel, the proclamation not simply of the teaching of Christ, but of Christ Himself, born, crucified, risen, ascended, the Saviour of the world. We are bound not only to affirm, but to show practically by patient effort that the faith is co-extensive with the interests of life; that it receives an intellectual expression in order that it may be applied effectively to conduct in the widest sense; that belief in the Incarnation —fulfilled in the Passion, the Resurrection, the Ascension, the mission of the Paraclete—supplies such an interpretation of the problems of creation as we are capable of receiving, and the help which we require, that we may be enabled to deal with them.

To this end the Christian Social Union proposes to its members three objects:

'1. To claim for the Christian law the ultimate authority to rule social practice.

'2. To study in common how to apply the moral truths and principles of Christianity to the social and economic difficulties of the present time.

'3. To present Christ in practical life as the living Master and King, the enemy of wrong and selfishness, the power of righteousness and love.'

These objects define broadly the foundation, the preparation, and the character of the active Christian life.

1. The conceptions which we form of God and man necessarily determine all we do. For Christians these two conceptions are indissolubly combined; and all mankind, all the world, are transformed for them under the influence of the fact that the Word became flesh. For Christians the ideas of the Fatherhood of God and the brotherhood of men are not merely magnificent aspirations, but direct interpretations of that central truth of history. We have, indeed, lost in part through an unhappy mistranslation the characteristic thought of the love of the brethren ($\phi\iota\lambda\alpha\delta\epsilon\lambda\phi\iota\alpha$), the feeling of Christian for Christian founded on the confession of one Faith; but the thought is prominent in the New Testament, and it is through the love of the brethren and through this alone that we can rise with sure conviction to the love of men as men. Our relation to God dominates and determines all other relations. The command to render to Cæsar the things that are Cæsar's is not a contrast to the command to render to God the things that are God's: the special duty is an embodiment of the universal duty. There can be no division in life: all life is essentially religious or irreligious. We accept literally as our rule of conduct, however imperfectly we may be able to fulfil it, the two commands: *Whether ye eat or drink, or whatsoever ye do, do all to the glory of God;* and *Whatsoever ye do, in word or in deed, do all in the name of the Lord Jesus, giving thanks to God the Father through Him.* We are our message; and in things great and small we are called upon to seek to make God known, that

is, to seek 'His glory,' and this can only be by realizing our own fellowship in His Son, as He has been revealed to us. All the conditions of labour and trade and social intercourse, of civil and national life, can be made conformable to a divine standard, and it is our duty to strive towards this issue.

2. The task is not easy, and can never be finally accomplished. The foundation fact of the Incarnation expresses perfectly, in terms of human life, our goal, our way, our strength; but it is also inexhaustible. No age and no race can master all its lessons. It offers something new for us to discover and to do, answering to the new conditions of the time. The Holy Spirit sent in Christ's name—sent, that is, to make His nature and His will better known—still takes of that which is His and declares it to us. We are set face to face with a living and speaking God. We are bound, therefore, to take account of every aspect and grouping of facts in the light of the Faith; and 'to study in common,' bringing together our differences of temperament and experience and knowledge, how to apply the Faith to the difficulties of our own time. This 'studying in common' is the central characteristic of the Union, and includes a promise of spiritual help to calm, systematic, scientific thought. The noble Jewish saying, that when two friends engage together in reading the Law, the Shekinah is added as a third, has for us a present application; and we may humbly trust that when two or three are gathered together in Christ's name ($εἰς\ τὸ\ ὄνομα$) to realize more perfectly in life what He is, He will

be in the midst of them. With what reverence therefore, with what patience, with what courage, with what hope, shall we labour together, if we realize that most holy Presence, before which the storms of earthly passion are stilled, accepting the discipline of delay, if delay be necessary, in order that all the truth may be gained. Every conclusion and every design which we form will be shaped in the spirit which England has retained from the movements of the sixteenth century, with a solemn sense of personal responsibility, with a passion for truth, with a whole-hearted devotion to righteousness.

3. At the same time all study will be directed to service. We believe in the ascended and living Christ. It is through us He works. The Vine bears fruit through the branches. In the bold language of early mystics, He needs us even as we need Him. In His name we hasten His kingdom. Yet even here we must remember that the weapons of our warfare are spiritual; and on great festivals, when we meditate on the conditions of our work,* we gladly recall that the earliest offerings which the Lord received were earthly treasures, brought by Gentile hands, that there is an eternal element in things transitory, that there exists already by Divine appointment a fellowship between the seen and the unseen orders.

We look beyond all present attainments, but,

---

* 'Members are expected to pray for the well-being of the Union at Holy Communion, more particularly on or about the following days: The Feast of the Epiphany, the Feast of the Ascension, the Feast of St. Michael and all Angels.'—*Objects of the Union.*

none the less, our faith constrains us to do whatever lies within our power to overcome selfishness and wrong. It is for Christians to form an intelligent, vigorous, and just public opinion. Legislation must be prepared for before it can be wisely carried. Legislation carried by force is not only ineffective, but demoralizing. The best cause, no doubt, cannot be gained without suffering. *We must through many tribulations enter into the kingdom of God.* But considerateness will avert many losses. The right is rarely all on one side. We shall, therefore, seek to understand, and, if possible, to know personally those from whom we differ; and in conflicts our prayers will be such as our adversaries, if honest and upright, might join in using. No fear of personal consequences will induce us to dissemble our convictions; and no hope of a premature advantage will induce us to dishonour them. 'It is not,' Lord Lawrence said, in words which have a wide application, 'the doing Christian things which creates irritation, but the doing Christian things in an unchristian way.'

The bond which holds the Union together is not the acceptance of a definite policy, but the acceptance of definite obligations resting on the one Faith. The Union has no programme which the members are required to maintain; it has principles which they are required to embody according to their knowledge and experience with sober and self-denying devotion, equally far from faithlessness and from self-assertion.

In this light the limitation of the Union to Churchmen is a pledge of breadth not less than of definiteness of faith; and it would be fatal to its work if it were to become identified with any ecclesiastical or political party. The better order at which we aim must correspond with the amplitude of our inheritance; the future which we strive to shape must be the crown of the past. Some among us may naturally be stirred to impetuous action by the sight of evils which come upon them with sad surprises. During the fifty years through which I have watched the advance of national, social and industrial reforms, I have gained the patience of courageous hope, which still grows stronger in the actual stress of conflict. Let the ideal be duly fashioned and loyally held and pursued, and little by little it will be surely established.

B. F. DUNELM.

LOLLARDS' TOWER, LAMBETH,
March 19*th*, 1894.

CONTENTS.

	PAGE
NATIONAL PENITENCE. Rev. Canon HENRY SCOTT HOLLAND	1
SOCIAL WARNINGS FROM HISTORY. The Very Rev. G. W. KITCHIN, D.D., Dean of Winchester	12
WASTED LIVES. Rev. A. F. W. INGRAM (Head of Oxford House, Bethnal Green)	22
AM I MY BROTHER'S KEEPER? Ven. Archdeacon FARRAR, D.D.	28
ETHICS OF PROPERTY. PART I. Rev. R. L. OTTLEY (Principal of Pusey House, Oxford)	38
ETHICS OF PROPERTY. PART II.	49
COMMERCIAL MORALITY. PART I. Rev. J. CARTER (Gen. Sec. C.S.U.)	59
COMMERCIAL MORALITY. PART II.	65
WAGES. Rev. Professor CUNNINGHAM	73
THE UNEMPLOYED. Rev. Canon BARNETT (Warden of Toynbee Hall)	84
WOMEN'S WORK. Rev. E. HOSKYNS (Rector of Stepney)	91
SPECULATION. Rev. WILFRID RICHMOND (Author of 'Economic Morals').	100

	PAGE
SOLDIERS AND SAILORS. Rev. R. R. DOLLING (Head of Winchester College Mission, Portsmouth)	110
BETTING AND GAMBLING. Rev. J. S. BARRASS	120
MARRIAGE LAW. Rev. Canon HENRY SCOTT HOLLAND	126
RELIGIOUS EDUCATION. Rev. G. W. GENT (Principal of St. Mark's Training College, Chelsea)	138
VAIN OBLATIONS. Rev. T. C. FRY (Headmaster of Berkhamsted School)	147
RECREATION. Hon. and Rev. E. LYTTLETON (Headmaster of Haileybury)	155
THE IMPERIAL CHRIST AND HIS DEMOCRATIC CREED. PART I. TOWN PROBLEMS. Very Rev. C. W. STUBBS, Dean of Ely, Author of 'Christ and Democracy'.	164
THE IMPERIAL CHRIST AND HIS DEMOCRATIC CREED. PART II. VILLAGE PROBLEMS	178
COMMON SENSE IN RELIGION. Ven. Archdeacon WILSON	188
SOCIAL HOPE. Rev. Prebendary EYTON (Rector of Holy Trinity, Upper Chelsea)	192
THE SOCIAL OUTLOOK. Rev. Professor H. C. SHUTTLEWORTH (Rector of St. Nicholas Cole-Abbey)	199

NATIONAL PENITENCE.

BY

CANON HENRY SCOTT HOLLAND.

'*Cursed is he that removeth his neighbour's landmark. Cursed is he that perverteth the judgment of the stranger, the fatherless, and the widow, etc. Cursed are the unmerciful. Amen.*'—DEUT. xxvii. 17.

CHRISTIANITY is often charged with depreciating the virtues of the good citizen. It has thrown, we are told, all its emphasis on holiness rather than on justice, on purity rather than on truth. It has its home in the inner mysteries of the spiritual life, in the unseen struggles and aspirations of the soul; to it the outer circumstances of the visible and social environment are matters more or less indifferent. And more especially will this inward tendency, we might say, declare itself at a season of penitence such as Lent, when the spirit of the man is sent back upon itself, to explore the inner recesses of his will, and to sift and analyze his deep-seated motives, that he may examine himself and confess his sin, and enter into the shadow of self-humiliation. That is what is meant by the religious season of Lent; that is what the main mass of devout believers intend by their Lenten exercises; and the earnest social reformer, even if he can allow all this penitential trouble to be spiritually valuable, cannot but ask whether it is calculated to create or to invigorate the strongest type of the good citizen at his work in the big world. Can the two interests hang together? Do the two cities correspond—the city of man on earth that now is, and the City of God, the Bride of the Lamb?

Anyhow, our Prayer-Book has a very clear idea that they do. It has, indeed, a great deal to say in Lent about sin, and penitence, and confession, and pardon, and all the mysteries of the soul at war with itself. It would dedicate its Lent largely to those invisible struggles in which a spirit wrestles all night in some black loneliness of agony, face to face with the nameless God whom it will not let go until He bless. Nevertheless, it deems it part and parcel of this same spiritual process to start off at the opening of Lent with the demands recorded in my text. Plain and straight enough, these rough, homely words. No unearthliness about them! We are not wafted off into any mystical world, strange and vague and intangible and remote, hovering, faint and fair, before our secret imaginings. No, indeed! very near it lies, this world of which they speak. Very obvious and very matter-of-fact these obligations that they press home. It is not a question that concerns some future condition of the soul in the sacred bliss of heaven; but what is its state to-day? What is it doing at this hour? What will it be about to-morrow? The entire concern is with positive, outward, undeniable facts, not with inward temper, or moods, or emotions. It is our acts that are arraigned. And these acts are all of them social; they are acts done by us to or towards our neighbour; they are the acts of citizens living under the close and incessant responsibilities of an organized society.

With these your Lent ought to begin. So the Prayer-Book says. Here is the door through which to pass in within the recesses of the Divine humiliation. If you want to draw nearer this year to the blood-sweat of Gethsemane, and to the bitter cross of Calvary, and at last to the holy sanctuary of your Easter feast, then there is one inevitable inquiry which blocks the way. It is perfectly simple, and no one can mistake it. It is this : What sort of citizen are you ? What kind of neighbour have you been ? Do you rob ? Do you lie ? Do you remove your neighbour's landmark ? Have you perverted the judgment of the widow, or the fatherless, or the stranger ? Have you smitten your neighbour secretly ? Have you taken reward against the innocent ? Have you been unmerciful to the helpless ? Have you extorted your gains from the weak and ignorant ? Have you used craft or force to win your own ends ? Have you ground down the poor ? Have you wrecked the bonds of marriage or of the family for your own evil passions ? Have you poisoned the moral atmosphere by your uncleanness ? Have you sinned against the brotherhood by slander or malice or falsehood ? If so, and if this is still your choice or portion, then you are under a curse—the curse of God. You are banned and barred. No Christian Lent for you ! There is no way open into the consolations or the gifts of religious life. The curse is on you ; your spiritual life is blighted, your soul is in prison, your strength is sapped, your claims and your rights before God are stripped off you ; you are a marked man ; you may not belong to the company of those who go up to the sanctuary of God ; you are cast out, branded, set apart, a felon. You must purge yourself of this charge, of this crime, if you are to enter the ranks of the loyal citizens of the Kingdom who have passed out of the darkness of the world into the light of the Divine society. This is the godly discipline which you profess through the Church your desire to restore. You must be prepared with your deliberate '*Amen*' to join with the whole assembly in pronouncing your own curse on all such social sin.

Ah! but, you say, this rough plain speaking misses its aim after all, misses it by its very rudeness. It belongs to primitive, to barbaric days of early Judaism, when men sinned with a strong hand and with a brutal frankness. They went at it with a cart-rope. And in the Prophets and Psalms, as we know, we are taken back to days when the public conscience had no definite standard of principle that it could enforce. A bad man was not ashamed to make his villainy his open rule of life. He deliberately set himself to rob, to take advantage of the weak, to pillage the widow and the orphan, to lie with his neighbour's wife. There was nothing to make him afraid or abashed. But now only professed criminals act like that. What is the use of attacking us with bare and raw challenges of this kind? Of course, we should not be here in Church, we should not be preparing to keep the Christian Lent, if we were not ready to lay our bann on murder and stealing and adultery and extortion. A light task this that you ask of us, to come here to church to-day, and pronounce other people accursed. We could do that much with an easy conscience. Where would be the profit? Is it not rather cheap? Has it nothing of the Pharisee about it, to stand up here and thank God that we are not like those wicked publicans who lie and cheat and rob?

That is a very pertinent question; and if we had nothing in view but our own separate individual lives, it might be difficult to recognise the bearing of the curse upon ourselves. But, my brethren, we none of us stand alone. Each is a member of a class, of a sect, of an interest, of a trade, of a Church; and nothing is more noticeable and startling to all who are anxious over social miseries than the discovery of the selfishness, the recklessness, the cruelty with which a class, or a sect, or an interest, or a trade, or even a Church, is capable of acting. We do in the mass what no one of us would consent to do on his own responsibility—nay, what each one of us would hotly repudiate.

A COMPANY HAS NO CONSCIENCE.

Let us take it in the case of a Company or a Board. We know how easily it all happens. The responsibility for the action taken finds no lodgment anywhere, has no seat of judgment, no Court of Appeal. No one knows with whom exactly the responsibility lies. It is shifted from shoulder to shoulder, until the last man, finding no other to whom he can pass it on, drops it quietly off into some ditch. And it is no one's business to note its disappearance. There is no audit on the side of conscience, no annual report in the company's books how it fares. Everybody supposes that somebody else is looking out to see that nothing is wrong; or else they may have settled down to a practical belief that morality is not the affair of a company, of an industry, or of a corporation; in the familiar and most wicked phrase, 'A company has no conscience.' Such societies must seek their own interests; they cannot spend their time in inquiring how their neighbours would be affected by their action. They have enough on their hands already in determining the conditions of their own success, which is their proper business. How can a railway company or a joint stock bank have moral obligations beyond those elementary principles of honesty without which trade itself could not exist? How can they be saddled with duties to their neighbours as well as to themselves? So we all murmur palliative phrases to choke down the sense of discomfort with which we now and again find that we ourselves have reaped profit from some course of action which has sweated down some miserable workers into infamous conditions of toil and life; or has made home for them unknown and impossible through the long hours that we have mercilessly imposed upon them; or has given them over to heartless death under chemical poisons, through sinful neglect of the precautions which one touch of human nature would have made imperative; or we have been dependent for our dividends upon casual and disorganized labour, which was inevitably bound to demoralize all who were concerned in it; or have got rents from slums which were a sanitary disgrace and a moral degradation; or from public-houses which fatten on the hideous drunkenness which their blazing gas and roaring heat fanned nightly into fever.

Ah! is there no room here for a plain, straight curse upon the sins that are open, on the sins that are reckless, on the sins that are savage? And yet they are sins which we in some corporate capacity too often aid and abet. As we review the ugly work of wrong, let us seriously ask ourselves, Is it against others only, and in no way against our own shamefaced selves, that we to-day pronounce, 'Cursed are they that make the blind to go out of his way, or taketh reward to slay the innocent? Cursed are the unmerciful, fornicators, and adulterers, covetous persons, idolaters, slanderers, drunkards, and extortioners. Cursed is he that putteth his trust in man, and taketh man for his defence, and in his heart goeth from the Lord.'

We may sin but too easily, through the irresponsibility of companies; or, again, we sin through becoming the tools of a system.

COMMERCIAL SPECULATION.

We all know how heartless, how mechanical, a System can become. Take commercial speculation. Take the money market. The men engaged in it are honest, kindly, and excellent. They propose to themselves nothing that is not legitimate, according to the rules of business. Yet the System itself that is created by their concerted efforts—what of it? What of its effects? How blind, how regardless, how inhuman may its workings be! How far it may carry us from all conceivable relations to moral responsibilities! As a System it is but too apt to take advantage of others' ignorance, of others' stupidity, of others' infirmities; it reaps its gain by others' vanity and greed; its normal work tends to exaggerate all fluctuations and uncertainties and disturbances of the money market, driving them into unnatural excess in order that the rapidity and extravagance of the variations may heighten the possibility of profits. As a System, it stamps down that which shows some signs of weakness, however temporary and accidental these may be, so that recovery is made impossible; it runs up anything that promises well into some unhealthy and inflated pre-eminence, and then hastily deserts it, before the terrible recoil follows which its own exertions have made inevitable, leaving the disaster to break on the foolish and ignorant, who had not wit enough to understand that they were following leaders who would be found to have withdrawn before the crisis came. My brothers, as we look round the English money market to-day, dare we say that there is no meaning for us in the curse on him who removeth his neighbour's landmark; on him who is unmerciful; on him who maketh the blind to go out of his way?

And classes, interests, professions—these all can commit gross sins from which any individual member of these would instinctively shrink. There is a horrible momentum which a vast profession or class may acquire—a momentum of accumulated self-interest. Always a profession makes in the mass for what is best for itself. It sustains an unceasing pressure in the one direction; it pushes its own way forward with the blind weight of a tide. Year by year, and bit by bit, it will go on piling up its resources; it never loses a step once gained, and never misses an opportunity for secret and solid advance. It thrusts aside by sheer pressure what obstructs; it beats under what is weaker than itself. It all happens by the sheer force of the situation. No one person in the profession or class exactly intends it; only each will tolerate on behalf of his class what he would never dream of doing on behalf of himself; and the volume of united selfishness is therefore ever moving on. And so it has come about that a great and honourable profession, such as that of the Law or of the Clergy, has, before now, found itself, to its own surprise, convicted, by the outraged conscience of its fellows, of injustice, harshness, greed, ambition. So a propertied class has before now come to build up its stability on some unhappy oppression; it has tolerated criminal miseries at its very doors without seeming to see that they existed. It has acquiesced in a condition which its own supremacy has made to seem familiar and natural, yet which every human-hearted member in the class would condemn with indignation if it was his *own* benefit which was bought at such a price. A class, an institution, has no eyes to see what its own prosperity costs to others. Thus it is that those social crimes have been committed which have been blotted out in revolution and in blood. Thus it is that the Church of Jesus Christ, founded in mercy and pity and loving-kindness, knit together in the love of the brotherhood, in the unity of the Spirit, in the bond of peace, has, as an organization, as a national institution, yielded so often in the Past to the impulsion of its own self-interest, and has suffered itself to arrive at a position which has made it become the very byword for arrogance and merciless ambition. All this has happened—we know it but too well; history records it over and over again with an iron pen graven upon rock for our warning.

TO-DAY'S ALARM BELL.

And can it be that this old story should, in any degree be repeating itself before our eyes to-day in

England? There is, at least, evidence enough to make us suspect ourselves. We all feel so innocent, so well-intentioned, so right-minded. Why, then, this cry of sullen hate which rises into our ears from those who suffer? Why should the cloud of dismay hang so heavy over England, our fair mother-land, the home of freedom, set as a jewel in the midst of the seas? Why do we fear to look our brethren in the face as the fierce war of competition clangs on and on in ruthless disregard; and the weak are crushed; and the old are forsaken; and the bitterness of misunderstanding sharpens our divisions? Why is it that this Church of ours, this Church of England, so dear to us, so rich in her catholic inheritance, so interwoven into England's story, so tingling with English blood; a Church, too, so teeming with activity, so fervent, so alive with prayer and worship—why is it that nevertheless she should somehow appear to the masses of English workers in country and in town, now at the very crisis of their fate, as if she stood aloof from their life, and was cold to their aspirations, and suspicious of their aims, and helpless in their needs; why should she wear the aspect to them of something privileged and propertied, jealous and timid, and carry with her so little of the likeness of Christ? Surely there is wrong here, wrong deep and large and gross, such wrong as may fall under a curse.

We can find no such wrong in ourselves. No; but we are members of the society which is thus at enmity with itself; members of a nation which is embittered by these heart-burnings; members of this Church which so fails to interpret and justify to the democracy the goodness of God the Father, the compassion and joy and strength of Christ our King. Look away to-day over the nation at large, and behold there the evil to which our selfishness contributes, the sorrow and the hate for which we must share the responsibility. It is our public burdens that we are summoned to assume. That which dishonours England is our personal dishonour. That which puts Christ to shame lies heavy on our souls. Let to-day be a day of national humiliation for presenting to God so disheartening a result of Christian civilization as that on which our eyes so sadly fall. Let us ask ourselves why we, as a nation, have lost so much of our national peace—our national confidence in the name of Jesus. Why has the curse fallen upon us, the curse of a divided house, and of paralyzed judgment, and of wounds that will not heal? Into each separate soul these questions must pierce like barbed arrows that cannot be withdrawn. Only according to the measure with which each solitary conscience takes home these things as matter of private personal concern, will the day of remedy dawn. True, it is not all wrong, not all black. There is earnestness in all classes, and patience, and moral soundness, and charitable zeal. There is a spirit of Christ-like devotion at work in the Church, that impels thousands of men and women into lives of mercy, that make for goodness and for peace. These are the salt that saves society from corruption. These keep alive the fire of sacrifice, and therefore of hope. But nothing of this should blind us to the terrible things still left undone, or should bribe us into murmuring 'peace' where peace has not yet been won. We are so tempted to let our good works, done in private, hide from us our public wrong-doings. And therefore it is that you and I are charged by the Church to face these tremendous arraignments at the opening of Lent. Therefore to-day we are each for himself, with trembling anxiety, to put the question to himself alone, Can it be that I, as member of a class, of a profession, of a trade, of a society, of a Church, of a nation, have indeed ministered in any way to this curse? Can it be that unawares, in negligence, in culpable disregard, I have wrung gain out of the weak, or have shifted my neighbour's landmark? Have I aided in perverting the judgment of the fatherless and the widow? Have I joined hands with the unmerciful and the extortioner, and the covetous, the drunkard, the adulterer? If I have, God be merciful to me a sinner; God be merciful to the nation and the Church that sinned in me! O Lamb of God, that taketh away the sins of the world, have mercy upon us! Grant us Thy peace!

SOCIAL WARNINGS FROM HISTORY.

BY THE

VERY REV. G. W. KITCHIN,
DEAN OF WINCHESTER.

'Behold, this child is set for the falling and rising up of many in Israel; and for a sign which is spoken against.'—LUKE ii. 34 (R.V.).

FROM the very dawn of Christianity, when Simeon took our Saviour, a little sinless babe, in his arms, down to to-day, throughout the whole range of the history of Christianity, this has been the keynote of the strife—'Set for the falling and rising up of many in Israel, and for a sign which is spoken against.' There is no delusion about Christianity. It is a common thing with those who think ill of our Faith to tell us it is based upon a delusion. It is no such thing. Christianity is firmly based on a Divine knowledge of the characteristics of the human being and of human nature, and a determination—which the Church has often forgotten, often neglected, often turned its back on—that nothing in human nature shall be glozed over, or put on one side, or pretended to be good when it is bad; but that from the beginning to the end, from then till now, the same choice between God and mammon, between God and sin, between God and selfishness, between God and what we call the devil, this same test, this same choice, is laid before mankind to take or to refuse, and woe to him who refuses the right and chooses the wrong; and God's blessing upon him who in the critical moments of his life knows how to choose the right and set the wrong boldly and bravely on one side.

The reason we keep Lent is not the old-fashioned reason at all. The reason is this—we are determined to bring before our fellow-countrymen, our brethren, those matters with regard to the Christian faith which are too apt to be forgotten, beginning, of course, with that most solemn question of all, How far has Christ's Gospel, how far has the little Babe of Bethlehem, been or not been accepted by us? Then the question—How far in God's providence, and by our efforts, poor and feeble as they have been, have we endeavoured, and has the Church through the ages endeavoured, to carry out the true principles of the salvation of man by Christ; the true principle which Jesus Christ taught when He came into the world, God and man, in order that He might lift mankind to a higher level, in order that we with Him might rise in this world to a nobler state and to heavenly places?

That is the rising; and what is the falling? The history of the Church is constantly teaching us the reply to that question. For the Church is continually falling—I care not who may be staggered at such a word as that—is it not true? Have we not here the very institution, the great home of the life of God in Christ, this very Body of Christ continually tending downward instead of soaring heavenwards?—though, God be thanked, if we trace the story of it through the ages, we discern that it does slowly rise, lifting with it the heavy reluctant burden of society. Everyone who has even for a moment meditated on the historical problems which differentiate modern Europe, modern life, the modern world, from the old world; everyone who in the light of our present day tests the whole history of Christianity, is filled with an awful sense that there is something that has gone quite wrong, that there is something in Christianity which has not met the difficulties, which has not overcome evils, which has not moved with the times, which has often failed to raise mankind to a higher level.

We yearn to be sure, my friends, with all our hearts, that here, in the Church of Christ, is hope for the present, and hope for the future; but above all things let me urge you, as you care for things heavenly, not to think that things heavenly are to be cut asunder from things earthly. For it is true that the 'kingdom of heaven is within us'; it is not that the kingdom of heaven is some external force acting on us from without: it is that God's Holy Spirit has entered into our hearts and has made a home and a blessing for us and for all whom we can influence.

DWELLERS IN CAVES.

I am glad this morning to be called on to speak to you about what are called the Social Warnings from History. There are such a number of them that it is almost impossible to do more than take two or three of the more salient and more prominent of the series; and with these I must content myself in the short time at my disposal. I have already spoken to you of our Saviour in Simeon's arms. That was a social warning of the deepest kind, in that we are called upon by the very existence of the Christian faith to choose between good and evil; this lies at the very foundation of all social progress. All social progress means in its very essence the progress of the individual. No doubt, social progress, backed up by legislation, by public opinion, and by those aids with which we endeavour to strengthen what is good within us, affects in the ultimate result the character of the individual. It is that the man has learned, God helping him in his work, to choose the good and to refuse the evil. It is that the man has said, ' My life, God being with me, shall be strong. and shall be pure, and shall do no wrong to my neighbours, and shall not take part in any of the cruelties or dark deeds of the world; but shall be spent as in the sight of God, because God has given me of His Holy Spirit, because God has saved me in the sacrifice of Christ.' And unless this result is well marked and frequent, in other words, unless it can be seen to raise and strengthen the individual man, and unless the Christian society can boast truly that it has given fresh life to the independence, the self-control, the instinct of justice, of mercy, of purity, within the individual, society will be on the downward path, and the light of the Gospel must have suffered some dark eclipse. When Christ called His followers 'the salt of the earth,' He told them that the individual was more than the society; they must always act on each other; that community in which the body politic weakens or obscures the individual is in an evil plight.

Now, soon after the Church had begun to feel its feet in the world, not very long after the death of the last of the Apostles, there came a time—those were not good times in the world's history, for the world was very corrupt—when men fervent for Christ, earnest persons if ever there were earnest persons, Christians to the back-bone, made this tremendous mistake—I do not suppose that any of you are likely to do the same—they thought that they could best get to heaven by cutting themselves off from their fellow-creatures; they made the mistake of going out into the wilderness as hermits; they made the mistake of saying that all the desires, all the tendencies, all the characteristics of this frail human body of ours are bad things, and have nothing good in them; 'we will, therefore, macerate ourselves, we will live apart from men, we will dwell in a cave, we will eat the scanty root, we will drink water when we can get it, and ask for nothing else.' In all these points they determined to cut themselves away from their fellow creatures, and to have no more to do with any human being whatever, and thus they hoped to get leisure in which to cultivate their spiritual nature. That was the first turning away from the true principles of Christianity.

For our dear Lord went in and out doing good; He touched the leper, He raised the fallen, He healed the wounds of the suffering; He was always with those who wanted Him most. And yet no sooner was He gone than a whole school of Christian people turned away from the true principles of Christianity, and lived selfish lives, caring only for themselves, thinking only of their own souls.

Is that a class of people which has entirely vanished in these days? I think not. We do not expect, when we go into the wilder mountains of Switzerland or elsewhere, to come suddenly on a cave in a mountain-side, and there see an emaciated saint working out his own salvation. No such thing as that. Still, in the very heart of English life, as we see it moving round us, do we not find hundreds of people who have made up their minds to get to heaven, but who have lost the road, thinking that heaven is to be gained only by cutting themselves away from the interests of their fellows, by taking no share in social responsibilities, by standing always in direct opposition to what in their enthusiasm they call 'the world'? We are in the world, but we need not be of the world. Be not of the world, but always in the world—that is Christ's message to us. This is my first social warning: let us never take part with those who think that the conditions of their brothers' lives are as nothing to them in comparison with the securing of their own salvation. No man ever got to heaven by planning it for himself alone. No man ever got to heaven by forgetting his brother.

WHO IS THE CHURCH'S ALLY?

The next social warning we may take is that which is afforded us by the time of Constantine. When the Church of Christ became an Established Church, when it became the friend and companion of great princes, when it took the lead in the world as the understood and recognised religion of the Western world, there was great danger connected with that too. To go into the details would take too long, nor do I desire to enter on any of the more thorny of the controversies raging in our day, and likely ere long to become matters of acute strife. I will, however, say this: the fact that the Church attached herself to the princes of the world led to her immense influence, and led at the same time to her great loss. For when those strong children of nature, the Germanic tribes, overwhelmed the disorganized and corrupted Roman Empire, then it was that the Church of Christ for the first time became distinctly the Church of War as opposed to the Church of Peace; and that stain on the Church of Christ—that she blessed war instead of ensuing peace — has clung to it from that day to this. It made the tremendous mistake of attaching itself to the powers of this world instead of trusting only in the strength of the Spirit of God. The Church of Christ should have remembered that God's Spirit, and God's Spirit only, can carry us safely through the changes and chances of this mortal life. They did not sufficiently recognise this; instead, they relied on the support and patronage of the princes of the day, on the great warrior, on the great monarch. 'Whosoever will save his life shall lose it; and whosoever will lose his life for My sake the same shall save it,' is a text which is worth a great deal of thought. For the Church went near to losing her soul when, for the sake of protection and influence in those turbulent days, she placed herself under the ægis of the war power of the Germanic conquerors. We need to take warning from the social evil of attaching ourselves to the strong, to the great of this world, rather than to the Spirit of God.

The next warning, on which we may only touch, is that arising out of the Reformation. I am one of those who think that the Reformation of the sixteenth century was a real blessing. Nevertheless, there is no doubt that at the period of the Reformation a great many evils crept into the

Church. Above all, there was one element which, though not altogether lost, fell into the background (and I may say in passing that in Christianity, as in all human life, doctrines, opinions, movements rise and fall, grow up and die down); this was the recognition of the work of God's Spirit in the Church and through the Church. The reformers of that time, by clinging to certain Biblical doctrines which were certainly true, and by shutting their eyes because of the prevalence of overlying superstition to others which were equally true—the reformers seem to me to have lost sight of the highest and most spiritual of all the elements in the corporate life of the Church.

A CHURCH THAT FELL.

Coming nearer to our own time, we have a startling warning from the evils which led to the French Revolution. That was a time when France, that had been in the van of civilization for at least two centuries, was definitely called on to answer this question, 'Has the Christian religion, as you know and understand it, power and life in it to mould the new elements of society in a way that shall be wholesome and permanent and good?' And to this question, which is certain to be asked of Christianity at every crisis of opinion, at every period of civil disturbance, at every time of social growth, when new forces come into play, when life enters on fresh phases, and it is a matter of 'old wine in new bottles,' came the unhappy answer, 'No!' The Church had lost the power. Never was there such a No in the world's history; never such an occasion of the failure of the Church —of the failure of Christianity I will not say, but of the failure of the Church—as was seen in those tumultuous years when a new life was born to Europe.

There were two kinds of clergy in the France of the middle of the eighteenth century, the noble clergy and the peasant clergy. The noble clergy were a large and powerful body, drawn from the younger sons of the noble families of France. They all, more or less, took holy orders in order that they might get hold of the abbeys, and bishoprics, and all the advantages, the pickings, as we should now call them, that were to be got from an Established Church in that day. Never was it heard in that period that any man from the ranks, however able, had risen to be a great personage in the Church. The consequence was that the noble part of the clergy attached themselves completely to the Court, and to the noblesse, with which indeed they were closely connected: they were the sons, the nephews, the personal friends of the aristocracy; the same blue blood ran in their veins. And it was this body of clergy which to the outer world represented the Church of France.

When the Revolution came it was heralded by the voice of Voltaire. He took the side of the nobility. Though not himself of noble origin, he attached himself entirely to courts and great persons, and gave them the benefit of his brilliant wit, his scathing tongue. The new spirit had entered into him; he represented the proposed reforms 'from above.' Voltaire therefore spoke the new ideas as they were being conveyed to the noblesse; and his battle-cry was, 'Christ is to be crushed.' Christ and Christianity and the Established Church to him meant the same thing. To him it all represented the constant force of reaction and resistance, and his fierce cry became the oriflamme of the new war against the Church in France. When he raised this terrible standard against their faith, not a voice was raised by the cultivated clergy, nor any resistance made by the Established Church. It shuddered and sank down and died.

The other half of the clergy—nay, nine-tenths of the clergy—belonged to the peasant class, and had, for the most part, the charge of the country parishes all over the kingdom. These men were cut asunder from those in the higher ranks; they were in the deepest ignorance; they scarcely knew how to perform the daily services; they often scarcely knew the meaning of the words they used. Yet they were fond of their people, and some of them took a very wholesome and honourable part at the beginning of the movement of the Revolution; but they were helpless, because of the terrible drawback that they were ignorant, absolutely ignorant.

Voltaire was the prophet of the upper classes. A prophet of the common people also arose, and that was Rousseau. Rousseau taught a popular doctrine, the doctrine of affection, the doctrine of sentimentality, the doctrine of love of man for man, the doctrine that we are hearing perpetually at the present day in England. Rousseau preached this doctrine to the people of France; and where the Church obtained one hearer, Rousseau obtained a hundred. The result was that when the crash came the country clergy were also swept away, when the flood overwhelmed the noble clergy. The attitude of the Church at the time of the French Revolution was that of absolute helplessness to do or say one word on the subject of these great doctrines which lie at the foundation of the best social life; and which if they be neglected react with fearful force on us clergy, and on our flocks.

THE CHURCH AS LABOUR'S FRIEND.

I had meant, had there been time, to speak about the way in which the Church of England is bound in our day to pay the greatest heed to civil and social matters, and to stand forth as a friend and teacher of the people; for they greatly need wise guidance with regard to those social problems which are rising up continually about us, and are receiving daily, and justly so, more and more attention at the hands of the community. The people of this country received, as you know, their share of power some years ago;

it is a power which they are still learning how to use. Had the Church of England understood how to come to the forefront and make friends with the working man, for that is the bottom of it; had the Church of England been able to say with a clear conscience, 'All our heart goes with those who work;' had she had the grace to say, 'Our leaders are of one mind with the workers of the country; the wage-worker is the man we want to raise, to teach him great principles, to teach him how to rule his house, and take part in public affairs'—if this had been our attitude, what a splendid thing it would have been for the Church of England! Then it might have been felt by men who have been alienated from us, that there is after all something good in the Church of England. God grant that it may not yet be too late; that we may still be able to show that we can rise to the duties of our day! Why should not the Church be able to repeat the words of Montrose when in his pride in and love for his country, and his strong self-reliance, he did not fear to say to Caledonia:

> 'I'll make thee famous by my pen
> And glorious by my sword'?

That is what the Church should say to the people of England: 'Famous by our pen'—by our learning, by our knowledge, by our being able to persuade men of the truth; and 'Glorious by the sword'—the sword of the Spirit, by which we will choose the good and avoid the evil, with which we will go forth in the power of God, smiting with a good courage at the devil, and showing that it is our religion to be the champions of the weak, the friends of the wage-earner, the true 'St. George for merry England.'

WASTED LIVES.

BY THE

REV. A. F. W. INGRAM,
HEAD OF OXFORD HOUSE, BETHNAL GREEN.

*'For what shall a man be profited,
if he shall gain the whole world and
forfeit his life? or what shall a man
give in exchange for his life?'*—ST.
MATTHEW xvi. 26 (R.V).

THE mystery of life is as great a mystery as ever. Men in these days are apt often to dislike mysteries, and to say that they cannot believe in the miraculous. But we men all believe in one miracle, the greatest break in the uniformity of Nature ever known—the gift of life, and we all accept one mystery —the mystery of life. Though we cannot define that mystery, we see that the gift of life is a sacred thing and a thing that we have no right to destroy in ourselves or to endanger in others; and we who live among working men cannot but regret that any effort designed to safeguard the lives of our friends should have failed from any cause.

But the subject given me to-day is even a more vital question than this, because it concerns the life of man as man. Man is not merely an animal. He has more than a physical life. It would be impossible for our Lord to have said that, 'Whosoever will save his physical life shall lose it; and whosoever will lose his physical life for My sake shall find it.' It is the life of man as man, as mysterious, but as real as the physical life, of which we are to speak to-day. Although we cannot define it, yet there are certain things we can see about it. We can see that it is independent of wealth. Give a man a chance in Bethnal Green, and he will live as true and deep a life as any man in Belgravia. We see that the life of man is independent also of popularity. The true man's life does generally win and attract, but it also may be crucified on Calvary. And as we see what that life is independent of, so also we see of what it is the secret. It is the secret, and the only secret, of rest to a man's conscience. You see a man restless, uncertain. What is the cause of his restlessness? He is not living the life which God has given him to live. This life is also the secret of power. Who are the men that have turned the world upside down but men like Lord Shaftesbury, who have lived out their lives to the full? Again, it is the secret of progress. Many a man starts in life with very moderate intellectual gifts, but by living his life to the full he often surpasses those who are far cleverer than himself.

And so we are forced to ask this question—in this extraordinary mystery of the life of man, which stands before everyone in this church to-day, are there any essentials that we can fix upon without which a man's life is a wasted and not a true one? I. The first—and I am careful as one who aims at being a social reformer to say it—the first essential of the true man's life is that it must be in communion with God. We call this, and perhaps rightly, the Church Forward Movement. But with all the failures of the Church in the past it has never ceased to be a witness to the unseen; and if we go into this great battle relaxing our hold on the unseen forces of strength, the Church Forward Movement will carry itself a very little way. We have to be in communion with God. Life comes from life in a spiritual as in a physical sense. And when you see a man who is now, perhaps, in middle life, giving up what his mother taught him—when you see a man thinking that busy philanthropy will make up for this first element in his life, you see him committing a fundamental mistake. Man is a praying animal, and he cannot help it. That is the first thing which distinguishes him from the mere animal. A man who represses or ignores that side of his nature is so far living a wasted life.

II. Secondly, if the life of a man is lived in communion with God, one characteristic of that life is that it must be pure. I am not speaking now of moral purity, but purity in business life and social matters. A man came to me the other day who lives in the East End of London, and who was earning up in this City four pounds a week. He said, 'I am forced, sir—it is my business—to do things which my conscience tells me are wrong. I am forced to make facsimiles, so called, which are not facsimiles. I have done it, but it is against my conscience, and I have come to tell you that I can do it no longer, and that I shall throw up my work.' He did throw it up. He threw up what our working men in Bethnal Green call 'splendid pay,' and I say that a man like that is an honour to the City. It is such men who will purify the morality of it. Do not think, my friends, that I am exaggerating in what I have said. In every mission instances occur of men coming and saying, 'I know this thing I am doing is wrong, but I have got a wife and children to care for, and I am forced to do it.' Now, if there is no other Lent resolve made by those who have been attending these services, there surely must be this one made, 'I will make it possible for every man in my employ to be a God-fearing man.'

A third great essential of a man's life is—and it is this that the Christian Social Union exists to demonstrate and enforce—that it should be lived in the service of others. One would have thought that to be an elementary truth, and that there would have been no need for any Christian Social Union to enforce it. But is there no such need? Surely, when we consider the matter—and I only repeat here to-day a question I have asked in all the great public schools of England, and at Oxford and Cambridge—is it credible that God should have given a small minority of this country wealth and leisure and education, and yet that they should imagine for a moment that they may spend it all on themselves? The thing is altogether incredible. 'Where is Abel, thy brother?' is the first question that will meet every one of us before the throne of God. 'Where is he? You were one of the minority; you had education and leisure, and wealth. But there was a life linked with yours; there was a young brother put under your charge, and it was an understood thing that those advantages were given to you in trust for him. Where is he? If you have spent them on yourself alone, he must be starving; if you have used up all the supplies, he must be fainting. Where is Abel thy brother?' We must face this question here and now if we are to face it at the last. We must face it in this city. There is at this moment a magnificent chance for men of all political creeds. We are not asking you to utter some party shibboleth, but to fulfil an elementary law of God. There is, I say, a magnificent opportunity at this moment that men of every kind, and of every colour of thought, can take to fulfil this law. A colleague of mine, whom I will not name, but who is himself a City man, occupies his time, after a hard day's work up here, at places which he has founded for the benefit of his brothers throughout East London, where they may receive that education and recreation of body and mind and spirit, which he in the bounty of God received himself. For what are these great clubs, which might be made of such tremendous power in that neighbourhood, languishing? For want of men to come forward and help. The working men in their committees are managing these places well, but they would be the first, if I called them up here, to tell you that what they need is men of education to help them in their classes and debates. While these great places, within a mile or two from here, are undermanned, I can never believe that this elementary truth of the Gospel has really penetrated the minds and hearts of City men.

Then again, during this last fortnight I have been to every college in Oxford. I have there addressed at least five hundred young men, and I can tell you that so far as they are concerned the heart of young England is sound. Where, then, is the difficulty? They are ready to give their lives to the service of God anywhere, but whenever any of them offer to do so, their relations, as a rule, hold up their hands in horror at the thought of them living and working, for instance, in East London. At this moment there are men at Oxford willing to endure what discomfort there is in living down in Bethnal Green, but they are opposed by their relations. I know that relations must look at all sides of the case, and that the father is thinking of his son's welfare in saying, 'I must not let my boy, in a moment of enthusiasm, wreck his career.' But are you parents so satisfied with your life as you live it? are you so satisfied that you have lived a man's full life, that you will check altogether your boy living a different one? We must be careful here, I know; let no hard word hurt the feelings of an affectionate parent who may be here; but still I say, Refrain from checking altogether this impulse of unselfishness; so far as may be, let them alone, lest haply you may be found even to fight against God.

Let us break, then, through the crust of old prejudice, and selfishness, and class feeling, and fling ourselves into a life of service for God and man. We do not want views, we want work. And as men work for God they will find their faith in Him strengthened, they will purify themselves more and more in their private and public life, even as God is pure, and they will *find* their lives. It is not, to quote again the often quoted illustration of a great preacher, it is not when a ship is fretting her side against the wharf that she has found her true life, but it is when she has cut the ropes which bind her to the wharf, and is out upon the ocean, with the winds over her, and the waters under her, it is then she knows the true joy a ship is made for, as she plunges and ploughs away the sea. And so it is not when a man is fretting his side against the wharf of his own self, not when he is saying, 'What will people think of me?' or 'How shall I get on?' but when he has cut the cords which bind him to his old self, when he is out on the ocean of loving work for God and man, with the winds over him and the waters under him, it is then he knows the true joy a man was made for; he has lost his life, as the world thinks, but in losing it so he discovers he has found it.

AM I MY BROTHER'S KEEPER?

BY THE

VEN. ARCHDEACON FARRAR, D.D.

WE hear much in these days of what is called the 'higher criticism'—in other words, of the application of critical, literary, historic methods to the documents and the narratives of Scripture. The method and its results are viewed by many with vague but unnecessary alarm. For this, at least, is certain, that no criticism can touch the spiritual depth, the moral instructiveness, enshrined in the pages of the Bible.

Whether the story of Cain and Abel be taken for literal history, or for profound allegory, there is not a line of it which does not breathe such wisdom as we could not parallel in the books of all the sages. In the envy of Cain; in God's revelation to him that every righteous offering will be accepted, but that the sacrifice of the wicked is abomination to the Lord; in the solemn warning that his peril lay in the wild beast of sin crouching at the door of his heart; in the rapidity with which the smouldering grudge broke out into the fiery wrath of murder, we have deep and abundant lessons. In the fact that so headlong was man's collapse from his original innocence that of the first two human beings born into the world the eldest grew up to be a murderer, and the younger to be his murdered victim, we have a terrible glimpse into that apostasy of man's evil heart, of which we see the bitter fruits in every walk we take in the common streets.

All national history, all war, every prison, every penitentiary; all riot, disorder, and sedition; that devilish type of manhood in which every other passion is merged into an incarnate rage; the deadly struggles of capital and labour; anarchy with its victims shattered by dynamite and its cities blazing with petroleum; incendiary tumults, the 'red-fool fury' of revolution, with its carmagnole and its guillotine—yes, the records of crime, and brutality, and suicide, and internecine struggle, which crowd our newspapers from day to day, are but awful comments on these few verses of the fourth chapter of Genesis, and indications of the consequences which follow the neglect of their tremendous lessons. All this, however, I must pass over, to fix your mind briefly on the fragment of the sequel.

Abel lay on the green grass, and earth's innocent flowers shuddered under the dew of blood. 'And the Lord said unto Cain, "Where is Abel thy brother?" And he said,'—for the first murderer is also the first liar —'"I know not"'; and he insolently added—for the first murderer is also the first egotist—'Am I my brother's keeper?' But the Lord sweeps aside the daring falsehood, the callous question. 'And He said, What hast thou done? The voice of thy brother's blood crieth unto Me from the ground. And now thou art cursed.' And Cain fled to the land of his exile, with the brand of heaven's wrath on his soul, and on his brow.

And here, my friends, I leave the narrative to speak to you of its significance for us all these millenniums afterwards. Briefly it must be, and very inadequately. All I can do is to impress a great principle; to deepen in our minds the sense of a solemn duty. Applications must be left to our own consciences and to other discourses. Yet there should be enough in the considerations which I would fain bring before you to awaken our serious thoughts. We each of us ask, in words and in our lives, 'Am I my brother's keeper?' God answers to each of us, 'You are!' The world, with all its might, answers, 'No! I am not.' Vast multitudes of merely nominal Christians—all those who are content with the dead Judaism of a decent, functional, and superficial religionism—all the vast army of the compromisers and the conventionalists—while they say, or half say, with their reluctant lips, 'Yes, I am my brother's keeper,' yet act and live in every respect as if they were not. There is little practical difference between their conduct and that of the godless world. Did not Christ indicate this when He described the two sons, of whom the bold rebel said, 'I will not go into the vineyard'; and the smooth, respectable hypocrite said, 'I go, sir,' and went not? Alas! we ordinary Christians are a very poor lot indeed. We have preached Christ for centuries,

> 'Until men almost learn to scoff,
> So few seem any better off.'

And if some, like the sneering lawyer, interpose an excuse, and ask, 'Who is my brother?' the answer is the same as that which Christ gave in the parable of the Good Samaritan. All men are our brethren; all who sin, all who suffer, all who lie murdered like Abel, sick and wounded like the poor traveller—where they have been left by the world's thieves and murderers, where they lie neglected by the frosty-hearted priest and the scrupulously sacrificing Levite on the hot and dusty wayside of the world.

Yes, all men are our brothers; and when we injure them by lies which cut like a sharp razor, by sneers, by innuendoes, by intrigues, by slander and calumny, by hatred, malice, and all uncharitableness, by want of thought, or by want of heart, by the lust of gain, by neglect, by absorbing selfishness, we are inheritors of the spirit of the first murderer.

But let us confine our thoughts to those who most pressingly need our services—to the great masses of the poor, the oppressed, the wretched, the hungry, the lost, the outcast. I will enter into no disquisition to account either for their existence or our responsibility for it. I will only say that among them lies, in some form or other, a great sphere of our duty, which, if we neglect for our pleasure, we neglect also at our peril. I need hardly pause to prove that this is our duty to our fellow-men, and above all to our suffering fellow-men. It is the unvarying lesson of Scripture. It is the essential message of the grand old Hebrew prophets. It was the frequent theme of Christ. It was the repeated exhortation of His Apostles and evangelists. We are constantly told by callous and worldly persons what a crime it is to give to a beggar; we are constantly lectured on our 'maudlin sentimentality' if we aid the starving families of men on strike. Even newspapers that are supposed to be specially Christian have no scorn too acrid for propositions dictated by a generous if perplexed sympathy for which they can find no better terms than 'verbal poultices,' 'sickly fluidity,' and 'hysteric gush.' One sees how summarily Isaiah and St. James would have been trampled into contempt by the trenchant criticisms of these gentlemen.

Well, let us by all means attend to our political economy, let us by all means tame down the splendid passion of the prophets, lest it should seem socialistic; and the generous impulse of the philanthropist, lest it should interfere with the ratepayer. But, in Heaven's name, let us not forget that, when all is said and done by those who rightly discourage mere casual dole-giving, the majestic claims of charity are not exhausted. We have not quite done our duty to the world of the wretched when we have proved to our own satisfaction that men whose passionate love for their fellow-men has reclaimed thousands of the arabs of our streets, and preached the Gospel to the lowest of the poor, are contemptible fanatics. Is it, indeed, the case that as we loll in our luxurious armchairs we not only need give nothing to help these efforts, but can even afford to look down from the whole height of our paltry conventionalism on workers who have more of the love of God and man in their little fingers than any ordinary thousand of us have in our whole loins? I esteem far higher the burning desire to help their fellow-men, the strenuous effort to carry that desire into effect, which actuates men who are the common sneer of worldlings and of religious newspapers, than I estimate the thin respectability and smug decorum of thousands of commonplace Churchmen. These lovers of their brethren have not only criticised and sneered—they have rescued the perishing, they have cared for the dying, they have healed the broken-hearted, they have wrought and fought, and toiled and prayed, and suffered. James Russell Lowell was a poet, a statesman, a man of the world. You know his poem, 'A Parable':

> 'Said Christ our Lord, "I will go and see
> How the men, my brethren, believe in Me."'

The chief priests, and rulers, and kings welcomed Him with state and with pompous services:

> 'Great organs surged through arches dim
> Their jubilant floods in praise of Him;
> And in church and palace, and judgment hall,
> He saw His image high over all.
> But still, wherever His steps they led
> The Lord in sorrow bent down His head;
> And from under the heavy foundation-stones
> The Son of Mary heard bitter groans.
> Have ye founded your thrones and altars then
> On the bodies and souls of living men?
> And think ye that building shall endure,
> Which shelters the noble and crushes the poor?'

In vain they pleaded their customs and their religious rites:

> 'Then Christ sought out an artisan,
> A low-browed, stunted, haggard man,
> And a motherless girl whose fingers thin
> Pushed from her faintly want and sin.

> These led He in the midst of them,
> And as they drew back their garments' hem
> For fear of defilement, "Lo! here," said He,
> "The images ye have made of Me!"'

The lesson is full of warning. That there is an almost shoreless sea of misery around us, which rolls up its dark waves to our very doors; that thousands live and die in the dim border-land of destitution; that little children wail and starve, and perish, and soak and blacken soul and sense, in our streets; that there are hundreds and thousands of the unemployed, not all of whom, as some would persuade us, are lazy impostors; that the demon of Drink still causes among us daily horrors which would disgrace Dahomey or Ashantee, and rakes into his coffers millions of pounds which are wet with tears and red with blood: these are facts patent to every eye. Now, God will work no miracle to mend these miseries. If we neglect them they will be left uncured, but He will hold us responsible for the neglect. It is vain for us to ask, 'Am I my brother's keeper?' In spite of all the political economists, in spite of all superfine theories of chilly and purse-saving wisdom, in spite of all the critics of the irreligious—still more of the semi-religious, and the religious press, He will say to the callous and the slothful, with such a glance 'as struck Gehazi with leprosy, and Simon Magus with a curse,' 'What hast thou done? Smooth religionist, orthodox Churchman, scrupulous Levite, befringed and bephylacteried Pharisee, thy brother's blood crieth to Me from the ground!' And this awful appeal which He is always making to us arouses a murmur, a hiss, a shout of reclamation. The respectable say, 'Are we rich, we clever, we refined people, we good Churchmen, we who thank God we are not as that fanatic, or that Dissenter, are we our brother's keeper?' And the scornful Nabobs say, 'What have we to do with these pariahs, these hangers-on of the gin-shops, these noisy demagogues?' Was not St. James thinking of such when, writing to the wealthy and religious respectabilities of his day, he sternly arraigned their callous selfishness with the charge, 'Ye have despised the poor'? There are many ways of asking the question of Cain. There is that of coarse ignorance; of men steeped in the greed and hardness of gold, who say outright, with Tennyson's 'Northern Farmer,' that 'the poor in a lump is bad.' But it may also be asked in a spirit which robs even charity of its compassionateness and makes a gift more maddening and more odious than a blow. Nor are they excusable who disclaim their responsibility to the world of anguish in the spirit of indifferent despair. How many find an excuse for doing practically nothing by saying, 'What good can we do? Of what earthly use is it?' And then, perhaps, they triumphantly quote the words of Deuteronomy, 'The poor shall never cease out of the land.' Ah, why do they invariably forget the words which follow : ' Therefore I command thee, saying, Thou shalt surely open thy hand unto thy brother, to thy needy, and to thy poor in the land. Thou shalt surely give him, and thine heart shall not be grieved when thou givest unto him, because that for this thing the Lord thy God shall bless thee in all thy works, and in all that thou puttest thine hand unto'? This despair of social problems is ignoble, and is unchristian. 'I know,' says Mr. Ruskin, 'that there are many who think the atmosphere of misery which wraps the lower orders of Europe more closely every day as natural a phenomenon as a hot summer. But God forbid! There are ills which flesh is heir to, and troubles to which man is born; but the troubles which he is born to are as sparks which fly upward, not as flames burning to the nethermost hell. The poor we must have with us always, and sorrow is inseparable from any hour of life; but we may make their poverty such as shall inherit the earth, and the sorrow such as shall be hallowed by the hand of the Comforter with everlasting comfort. We can, if we will but shake off this lethargy and dreaming that is upon us, and take the pains to think and act like men.' Once more, there is an unfaithfulness which does not, indeed, challenge God with the question, 'Am I my brother's keeper?' but in domestic sloth acts as if it were not. The poets, with that inspired insight which makes them the deepest of moral teachers, have seen this most clearly. Coleridge speaks of

> 'The sluggard Pity's vision-weaving tribe
> Who sigh for wretchedness, yet shun the wretched,
> Nursing in some delicious solitude
> Their dainty loves and slothful sympathies.'

Wordsworth sings that we are living in days

> 'When good men
> On every side fall off we know not how
> To selfishness, disguised in gentle names
> Of peace, and quiet, and domestic love.'

If it is only the basest men who are drowned and besotted in their own selfish and sensual individualism—the *égoïsme à soi*—many even good men and women have need to be seriously on their guard against the slightly expanded selfishness—the *égoïsme à plusieurs*—which wholly absorbs them in the interests of their own children, and their own families, till it blinds their eyes to the fact that they do nothing else. There is a serious danger to us all lest our narrow domesticity should gradually enervate many of our nobler instincts by teaching indifference to the public weal as a sort of languid virtue. 'I live among my own people.' Yes; but God made me also a citizen of His kingdom. 'Life,' said Lacordaire, 'when limited to itself borders closely upon selfishness. Even its very virtues, if they do not seek to extend themselves over a wider area, are apt to succumb to the narrow fascination it exerts.' Many a man, in his affection and service to his family, forgets that he belongs also to the collective being; that he cannot without guilt sever himself from the needs of his parish, of his nation, of his race, of the poor, of the miserable, of the oppressed. If he is to do his duty in this life, he must help them, he must think for them, he must sympathize with them, he must give to them. We must not be like the churlish Nabal, saying, 'There be many servants nowadays that break away, every man from his master. Shall I then take my bread and my wine and my flesh that I have killed for my shearers, and give it unto men whom I know not whence they be?' We must not be like Dives, arrayed in purple and fine linen, faring sumptuously every day, while Lazarus lies neglected —and, in all but vain words, unpitied—at our doors. The old Epicurean poet Lucretius says that 'it is sweet when the winds are sweeping the waters into storm, in some great sea, to watch the dread toiling of another from the shore.' The feeling of the Christian must be the very opposite to this. He must man the lifeboat. If he be too weak to row he must steer; if he cannot steer he must help to launch it; if he must leave even that to stronger arms, then

> 'As one who stands upon the shore,
> And sees the lifeboat go to save,
> And all too weak to take an oar,
> I send a cheer across the wave.'

At the very least, he must solace and help and shelter and supply the needs of the poor shipwrecked mariners. The meanest position of all and the commonest is to stand still and do nothing but chatter and criticize, and say that the lifeboat is a bad one and not fit to be used, or that it is being launched in quite the wrong way and by quite the wrong people. Worst and wickedest of all is it to stand still and call those fools and fanatics who are bearing the burden and heat of the day. The best men suffer with those whom they see suffer. They cannot allay the storm, yet, since the cry knocks against their very hearts, they would at least aid those who are doing more than themselves to rescue the perishing. They would at least sympathize and help, and, at the lowest, give. I commend these thoughts to your earnest consideration, and having set before you the general principle and the general duty, I conclude with a practical application. Of this we may be sure, that character, not creed, service, not form, is the test, and the sole test which, alike in the Old and New Testament, God invariably requires of us. It is love which is the fulfilling of the law. It is only by keeping the commandments that we can enter into life. We may come before God in the bluest of orthodox fringes and the broadest of Pharisaic phylacteries, we may belong to the only right organization, we may hold to the only right opinions about priests and sacraments, we alone may be careful about keeping the rubrics with the most scrupulous accuracy, but all this will be as valueless, nay, as hateful, in the sight of God, if it be unaccompanied by charity and service, as were the mint, anise, and cumin of the arrogant and exclusive Pharisees and priests who murdered the Christ for whom they professed to look. There is but one test with God of orthodoxy, of catholicity, of membership of the kingdom of heaven. It is given in the last utterance of Revelation by the beloved disciple. It sweeps away with one breath nine-tenths of the fictions and falsities of artificial orthodoxy and fanatical religionism. It is: 'He that doeth righteousness is righteous,' and 'He that doeth righteousness is born of God.'

THE ETHICS OF PROPERTY.

BY THE

REV. R. L. OTTLEY,
PRINCIPAL OF PUSEY HOUSE, OXFORD.

I.

And he spake a parable unto them, saying, The ground of a certain rich man brought forth plentifully:
And he thought within himself, saying, What shall I do, because I have no room where to bestow my fruits?
And he said, This will I do: I will pull down my barns, and build greater; and there will I bestow all my fruits and my goods.
And I will say to my soul, Soul, thou hast much goods laid up for many years; take thine ease, eat, drink, and be merry.
But God said unto him, Thou fool, this night thy soul shall be required of thee: then whose shall those things be, which thou hast provided?
So is he that layeth up treasure for himself, and is not rich toward God.—ST. LUKE xii. 16-21.

THE passage before us suggests a few general reflections bearing on the subject of property.

I. It implies that the institution of property is recognised by Jesus Christ; is sanctioned as a social arrangement which in principle is right. If the possession of property is an occasion of great sins, and great negligences, it is clear that the right use of it demands conspicuous virtues, and is fruitful in social and personal blessings. Thus sanctioned by our Lord, the rights of property have been made the subject of Christian thought in every age of Church history; and the time seems to demand a restatement of principles which are really old, but practically forgotten. Before, then, we consider some of the lessons contained in our Lord's parable, it will be well to state clearly what Christian teachers have held as to the ethics of property. They generally appear to confine themselves to the following points

1. There is a distinction between the law of Nature and the law of the State, or positive law. By the law of Nature all things are common to all men*; there is no such thing as a 'right' of personal possession. Indeed, the very idea of private 'right' can only be developed in civil society; it must be instituted, regulated, and protected by the positive law of a community. In fact, it is a creation of society, of human law. And St. Thomas Aquinas maintains that in the abstract it is possible for the law of Nature to supersede the positive law of the community. 'According to the natural order of Divine Providence,' he says, 'material things are ordained for the supply of human necessity.' And therefore, in a case of absolute necessity, the law of Nature justifies an invasion of the right of property, which by the very fact of extreme necessity is 'made common.' For 'the superfluities which belong to some are by natural right bound to be given (*debentur*) to the support of the poor.'† It is obvious that in a country living under a poor law, like our own, the abstract possibility contemplated by St. Thomas cannot be said to exist.

2. But abstract natural right is limited and controlled by positive law. For though, as Edmund Burke says, natural

---

* See references in Ashley, 'Economic History,' vol. i., p. 207.
† 'Summa,' ii. 2ae. 66, 7. Cf. Gury, 'Compendium theol. moralis, tom. i., p. 413 (Paris, 1868).

rights 'exist in total independence' of government, 'and exist in much greater clearness and in a much greater degree of abstract perfection'; yet 'their abstract perfection is their practical defect. By having a right to everything' men 'want everything. Government is a contrivance of human wisdom to provide for human wants.'* For its own benefit, therefore, human society is obliged to sanction and protect the institution of property. Thus, although some early Christian teachers were inclined to question the possibility of rights which they traced to human sin, yet later thinkers allow that property is necessary both on grounds of social expediency and of individual moral discipline. On the one hand, property is a necessary condition for the development of a country's resources, and a necessary stimulus to human exertion. The creation of wealth, the supply of natural wants, the organization of industry, the subdual of Nature to man's purposes, could not go on if rights of property were abolished. On the other hand, property is a necessary condition of a man's personal development. It is the material on which man as a moral personality exerts his energies, and displays his character. It is 'the best means hitherto devised of stimulating the individual's energies in productive work.'† The responsibility it imposes trains a man in prudence, generosity, self-control, humility, compassion, public spirit, and charity. Property brings him face to face with great moral duties; it opens the way to high possibilities in character. Because wealth and responsibility go together, 'wealth and Christ may co-exist.'‡ Christianity has no quarrel with property as such. Some of the noblest characters in the Gospel are men of wealth—Nicodemus, Zacchaeus, Joseph, the 'good man and just.'

* 'Reflections on the French Revolution,' p. 70 [ed. Payne, Oxf., 1883].
† Rev. H. Rashdall, 'Assize Sermon,' Nov. 9, 1893 (St. Mary's, Oxford).
‡ T. E. Brown, 'Studies in Modern Socialism,' p. 162.

3. Property is ultimately subject to the control of the community—of the State. It is acquired subject to the protection of the State. 'It is held in subordination to the supreme claims of the community.'* It is justifiable in so far as it is used for the benefit of the community. The right to enjoy wealth may be legitimately called in question by the State when that wealth is not serving a social purpose. Society, in short, can exercise a claim to regulate the right of property; in extreme cases, might altogether set it aside.† And this abstract principle is reinforced by a consideration of the conditions under which property is acquired in modern times. In the highly complex conditions of modern industry 'wealth,' it has been justly said, 'is the product of the whole society, exclusive of the idlers.'‡ Without the labour of countless hands, the protection of the State, the co-operation of innumerable agencies, making possible manufacture, exchange, and output, no wealth could accumulate in the hands of any individual. It is thus obviously true that property is, in some sense, created by the community, and therefore that it not merely owes duties to the community, but is indefensible except on condition that it renders service to the community. As a matter of fact, the control of the State over property has been continually asserted, and I am aware what far-reaching consequences might be deduced from the Christian principles stated above.

Such, then, are the broad principles on which property is recognised as a necessary institution by Christianity. The duty seems to be laid upon us at the present time of reviving the best traditions of the Church's moral teaching; by bringing the duties of property into the light of God; by reminding men of wealth that they are amenable to a higher law than that sanctioned by Parliaments and enforced by courts of justice.

* Lilly, 'Right and Wrong,' pp. 182, 183.
† For the bearing of this position on ecclesiastical property see the passage from Bp. Butler (Note A).
‡ Rashdall, *ubi sup.*

II. Let us now turn to our Lord's parable, and consider what it teaches as to the characteristic sins of the rich; let us notice also the nature of the judgment which, in a typical case, overtakes the misuse of wealth. This will be the subject of to-day's sermon.

1. The first and most obvious peril of the rich man is the sin of avarice: the inordinate desire of accumulation. To the 'rich fool' his property was the one centre of all his thoughts, hopes, and aims. 'What,' says he, 'shall I do?' (Observe that he uses the same anxious expression which, in another connection, is applied to eternal life: 'What shall I do to inherit eternal life?' in yet another case to the salvation of the soul: 'What shall I do to be saved?') The rich fool has no ideal, no aspiration, no desire, no hope for the future beyond the mere pleasure of acquisition. He is engrossed in the thought of the abundance of the things which he possesses. This is more than mere short-sightedness. It is fatal misdirection of desire: it is avarice—'covetousness which is idolatry.' Avarice means eagerness for gain beyond the limit necessary to a man's station in life;* and it is a sin against God and against society: a sin *against God*, because it implies the withholding of the heart from God; money becomes an idol, the making of money a religion; for 'that is truly a man's religion, the object of which fills and holds captive his soul and heart and mind—in which he trusts above all things, which above all things he longs for and hopes for';† and a sin *against society*, because wealth is a social good; to withhold it from doing service to our fellowmen is a breach of the eighth commandment; to hoard, conceal, or amass it beyond limit for private ends is in a sense to steal it.

Here, then, we have a characteristic Christian principle:

---

* 'Summa,' ii. 2; 118: 1 'Avaritia peccatum est quo quis supra debitum modum cupit acquirere vel retinere divitias.'

† Dean Church, 'Cathedral and Univ. Serm.,' p. 156. Cf. Col. iii. 5; Eph. v. 5.

the importance of due limitation in the acquisition of wealth. Yet Aristotle anticipates it to some extent when he says that sufficiency of wealth, if a good life be held in view, is not unlimited; and when he adds the remark that the tendency to limitless acquisition is eagerness for life, but not for good life.*

2. A second peril of the rich is selfishness in expenditure. The rich fool speaks of 'my goods, my fruits, my barns.' In the same way Nabal, the churl of David's time, says: 'Shall I take my bread and my water and my flesh that I have killed, and give it unto men whom I know not whence they be?'† The man makes self his centre; to him enlargement of wealth means not larger liberality in distribution, but increased luxury in personal expenditure. He has that perverted sense of the 'sacredness' of property which is not, we may fear, very uncommon. Property is indeed 'sacred': but in what sense? It is sacred because the use of it is subject to the moral law of God, and also because the possessor of it has a sacred right to protection in the fulfilment of his social duty. Property is not sacred in the sense that a man may do what he wills with his own. The Gospel, as we have seen, claims wealth for human society; demands its use as an instrument in the promotion of public wellbeing. The evangelical law supersedes the requirement of mere civil law. 'He,' says Wycliff in his treatise on Civil Lordship, 'who in accordance with human rights transgresses in the use of his riches the boundaries fixed by the law of the Lord, sins against the Lord.'‡ Here we have another Christian principle regulating the use of wealth; not the minimum which human law requires, but the maximum which evangelical law directs, is to be the measure of the right use of property.

* Aristotle, 'Politics,' i. 8, 14; 9, 16. See F. W. Robertson, 'Sermons,' second series, No. 1, 'Christ's judgment respecting inheritance.'
† 1 Sam. xxv. 11.
‡ 'De civili dominio,' lib. i. 20.

3. A third peril of riches is implied in the words of the rich fool to himself: 'Soul, thou hast much goods laid up for many years; take thine ease.' Notice here the fatal effect of misused wealth in the paralysing of moral and spiritual effort. Our Lord says in another passage recorded by St. Luke, 'Woe unto you rich, for ye have received your consolation.' Not on rich men as such is this woe pronounced; but on those who yield to the temptations of wealth—who are contented and at ease. Christ points to the danger of a growing insensibility to the claims and appealing needs of others; the gradual closing of the spiritual eye to all high objects of hope, love, and fear; the gradual hardening of the heart and conscience. It is related of Mr. Cobden that he once observed, 'When I go to church there is one prayer which I say with my whole soul: *In all time of our wealth, Good Lord, deliver us.*' The chief danger of large possessions lies in their power to blind, harden, benumb the spiritual faculties. Material comfort and luxury tends gradually to deaden the soul; to kill out all high aspirations; to form a crust about us which the calls to social service and helpfulness cannot pierce; to undermine entirely the sense of need and moral misery, to which faith in a Redeemer and Saviour can make appeal. In fact, the dangers of wealth are like those of an incessant life of business. There is a striking passage in St. Bernard's book addressed to Pope Eugenius III., in which he warns the Pope of the peril of being constantly immersed in the multifarious secular business which, in those days, pressed upon the occupant of the Roman see. He bids Eugenius beware lest all this mass of routine work should lead him whither he would not. 'Ask you whither?—to a *hard heart*. . . . And what is a hard heart? A heart neither broken by compunction, nor softened by pity, nor moved by prayers, nor yielding to threats; a heart ungrateful for benefits . . . inhuman in dealings with men, presumptuous towards God; a heart forgetful of the past, negligent of present opportunity,

blind to the future. . . . In one word—that I may sum up all the evils of this one dreadful evil—a heart that fears not God nor regards man.'* And surely we might add: 'So is he that layeth up treasure for himself, and is not rich towards God.'†

III. We have considered briefly the dangers of wealth which the parable sets before us. They might be described summarily in three words: avarice, that makes an idol of wealth; selfishness, that will not share its good things with others; sloth, that hardens the heart against the claims of our fellow-men. In very various degrees these sins are apt to beset the rich; and 'hardly,' indeed, 'shall they that have riches enter into the kingdom of God.'‡ But with God are possible the things which are impossible with men. If there is any class that needs more than others to cultivate by diligent prayer for God's grace the sense of dependence, of moral need, of responsibility, it is the class to which the rich man of the parable belonged. Many there are who rise victorious above these perils and hindrances; and, indeed, the very fact that he is subject to temptations so fierce gives the man of wealth a claim on the compassion and consideration of the poor. For the Gospel is not one-sided. It preaches a brotherhood of men, and brotherhood implies mutual obligations. Our Lord traces to one and the same root of covetousness the passionate cry, 'Speak to my brother that he divide the inheritance with me,'§ and the grasping selfishness which says, 'What shall I do because I have no room where to bestow my fruits?'

But let us turn our thoughts, in conclusion, to the message which comes to the rich fool from God Himself. In terrible contrast to his own words, 'Soul, thou hast much goods; take thine ease,' there comes to him the Word of God:

---

* 'De consideratione,' lib. i. 2.
† St. Luke xii. 21.
‡ St. Luke xviii. 24.
§ St. Luke xii. 13.

'God said unto him, Thou fool, this night they require thy soul of thee.' There is something very awful in this mysterious expression. What is meant we know not. Probably some sudden, swift catastrophe; an uprising among his servants; a nocturnal attack of robbers; an outburst of envy or disappointed greed among his underpaid *employés*; an act of revenge for some private wrong done to a poor man, such as Dickens describes so dramatically in his 'Tale of Two Cities.' You recollect how the Marquis—whose carriage, as it dashed through the streets of Paris, had killed a poor workman's child—arrives at his luxurious country seat, and at night goes to rest in a voluptuous chamber, softly carpeted and curtained, and composes himself to sleep. You may remember what they find in his room on the morrow. The face of the Marquis lies on the pillow cold and still. 'It was like a fine mask; suddenly startled, made angry, and petrified;' and 'driven home into the heart was a knife.' Some such end—so sudden, so fearful, so unprepared—may have been the death of the rich fool.

We know that in Europe generally, not least in England, there are strange symptoms of social upheaval and disturbance. Our highly-developed civilization has to protect itself against desperate men whom the conditions of modern society have maddened. And behind them the voice of millions of toilers, hitherto dumb, is rising louder in our ears. What is the root of our present danger—our present critical social state? Largely the abuse of the right of property. The sufferings and wrongs incident to the institution of property are indeed so aggravated that wild remedies are proposed; the institution itself is attacked. What wonder if men who are miserable and embittered, or full of passionate pity for the poor, cry aloud for the abolition of that which they hastily assume to be the source of all their evils? The most formidable symptom, it has been said, of social disorder is 'the growth of Irreconcilable bodies within the mass of the population. . . . Church and State are alike convulsed by them; but in civil life Irreconcilables are associations of men who hold political opinions as men once held religious opinions. They cling to their creed with the same intensity of belief, the same immunity from doubt, the same confident expectation of blessedness to come quickly, which characterizes the disciples of an infant faith.'* 'Wherever,' says another thoughtful writer, 'classes are held apart by rivalry and selfishness, instead of drawn together by the law of love; wherever there has not been established a kingdom of heaven, but only a kingdom of the world, there exist the forces of inevitable collision.'† So in touching upon the swift and mysterious fate of the rich fool, our Lord would perhaps teach us to consider what is the inevitable end of any social arrangements which are content to permanently disregard the moral law of God. If the institution of private property comes to mean in fact a violation of God's will; if it fosters in a man avarice, heartlessness, shameless luxury, and worldly ease that can make him contented and comfortable while thousands of his fellow-creatures are struggling for the bare necessaries of life—it is doomed. 'It is unjust; it cannot last.' The social state which is based on an iniquity cannot stand; it is nigh unto vanishing. The prophets warned the ancient world what a corrupt society must expect—a society that refused to be reformed. They were laughed at by their contemporaries; but we know who were right, and who were wrong. It was not in vain that they testified, 'Woe to the bloody city; it is full of lies and robbery.' 'Woe to her that is filthy and polluted, to the oppressing city'; woe, for 'the just Lord is in the midst thereof.' 'Woe to them that are at ease in Zion, and trust in the mountain of Samaria, which are named chief of the nations.'‡

* Maine, 'Popular Government,' p. 25.
† Robertson, 'Sermons,' first series, p. 247.
‡ Nah. iii. 1; Zeph. iii. 1, 5; Amos vi. 1.

Our hope for the future lies, surely, in siding with the Eternal Righteousness which 'spake by the prophets.' There is one social force which is not always taken into account, but which produces effects of acknowledged importance and magnitude. It is the power of awakened conscience. Among many social symptoms that seem threatening and disquieting, there is one that is full of hope and promise,—I mean the fact that there is an evident desire on many sides to bring our social evils into the light of Christ's Gospel; a desire to return to first principles; a desire to get God's will, in relation to modern problems, done on earth even as it is done in heaven.* To contribute by individual self-sacrifice and exertion to that one and only worthy end of human endeavours, is its own reward.

* Cf. Dale, 'The Ten Commandments,' p. 202.

THE ETHICS OF PROPERTY.

BY THE
REV. R. L. OTTLEY.
II.

'And he said unto them, Take heed, and beware of covetousness: for a man's life consisteth not in the abundance of the things which he possesseth.'—ST. LUKE xii. 15.

IN treating the subject of property, we may find it useful to adopt a distinction made by St. Thomas Aquinas between two things: (1) the right of acquisition; (2) the right of use. Clearly these do not stand upon precisely the same ground. As to the first, the right of acquiring personal property, we have seen that it claims protection from society as being absolutely essential to the creation of wealth and the development of industry; essential to the training of character and personality. The desire for acquisition is an original element in our nature; and human will necessarily seeks for itself implements. Accordingly, Aristotle defines property as 'a collection of implements for the purposes of life.'* The right to acquire is a necessary stimulus to human exertion; some nations are even deficient in desire for accumulation, and consequently in industrial energy.† In our own race the instinct of acquisition is perhaps inordinately developed; and it is not too much to

---

* 'Politics,' i. 4.   † Cf. Robertson, 'Sermons,' ser. 2, p. 13.

say that it is the source in great measure of our unhappy social condition; of the appalling contrasts with which we are so familiar in our great cities.

As to the *use* of property, however, we may notice that there is no question of 'rights' in any narrow individualistic sense. Christian teachers with one accord maintain that, as regards use, a man has no right to look upon any possessions as his own, but only as common to all, only as held in trust for the general good.* In other words, a man has no right to do what he likes with his own; he has only a right (which means a recognised duty) to do what he *ought* with his own. Once in the Gospel we find one who says, 'May I not do what I will with mine own?' but a moment's reflection will remind us that He who so speaks immediately adds, 'I am good.' Goodness alone can be trusted to do what it wills with its own.†

Here, then, we have two divisions of our subject. We may deal with the ethics, first, of acquisition; secondly, of use.

I. We ask, then, what are the principles that should guide and regulate the instinct of acquisition? And on this point the Gospel is perfectly explicit. Thus it teaches:

1. *That wealth is not the true end of man.*—' A man's life consisteth not in the abundance of the things which he possesseth.'‡ It is the primary duty of the rich to assert this principle in their own conduct, and to transmit it as a tradition to their heirs; to live, act, and speak so that the getting of wealth should cease to be regarded as the chief end of man. An American writer declares that 'the greatest work which the coming century has to do, is to build up an aristocracy of thought and feeling which shall hold its own against the aristocracy of mercantilism.'§ We

---
* Thom. Aquinas, 'Summa,' ii. 2ae, 66, 2.
† St. Matt. xx. 15.
‡ St. Luke xii. 15.
§ A. D. White, quoted by T. E. Brown, 'Studies in Modern Socialism,' p. 167.

are to discountenance the idea that money is to be the passport to social eminence. In America the disastrous effects of the purely mercantile spirit are said to be painfully apparent. 'It has created,' says one authority, 'a class of men in whom all finer traits of character are extinguished; whose aspirations are dwarfed; whose sympathies are destroyed; men benumbed in conscience, brutalized in feeling, whose right is might, and who know no law but the law of their own audacity.'* It is, in fact, the first principle of Christianity that a man's worth is to be estimated not by what he has, but by what he is; a man's well-being consists —and here Christian teaching contrasts sharply with some phases of materialistic socialism—not in the outward satisfaction of animal desires, but in a certain inward character; not in acquisition but in distribution: 'it is more blessed to give than to receive.'†

2. The Gospel says that wealth must be *justly* acquired. The money-making instinct is to be subjected to the law of righteousness. So the question arises, How do we come by our wealth? It is a question that may well make us uneasy, as we consider how far removed from the law of Jesus Christ is the standard which ordinary mercantile life allows. Clearly, then, the Gospel condemns accumulation of property by unrighteous means. A man is bound to ask himself, How have I become rich? If he has acquired that which belongs to another by false pretences, or without giving fair equivalent, he has broken the eighth commandment. What anxious heart-searchings this suggests! 'Have my gains been won at the expense of the spiritual and bodily lives of others? Have they been wrung from the toiler by unjust means, by payment of starvation wages, by getting the utmost exertion out of him at the minimum wage he can be induced to accept, by robbing him of all opportunity for moral and spiritual improvement? Have

* Brown, *op. cit.*, p. 166.
† Acts xx. 35.

I grown rich by fraud and false pretences, by turning out scamped work or inferior goods, by an unrestricted passion for purchase at impossible prices? If I am an owner of house-property, have I exacted my rents regardless of the sanitary condition of the tenements? Have I taken advantage of laws which are allowed to be a dead letter only by the apathy of public opinion? Or am I taking shares in a company which I perfectly well know makes its way by false representations and lying advertisements, which attracts by offering excessive dividends, and recognises no responsibility for the welfare of its *employés?* I need not carry on this line of thought, which has already been brought to your attention. At least, such reflections may awaken our conscience in this matter of acquisition. There are surely not a few who owe to the community a great act of *restitution*, like that of him who said, 'If I have done wrong to any man, I restore him fourfold.' A man need not leave his business if he sees his way to reforming the conduct of it; but two duties, on Christian principles, he certainly owes to society: reformation for the future, restitution for the wrongdoing of the past.

3. As to the limits of acquisition, the Gospel teaches the duty of *moderation.* Aristotle, as I reminded you, had already insisted on this point. The man who accumulates wealth beyond what is fairly needed for the maintenance of himself and his family, and real efficiency in work, lies under a heavy responsibility and is open to great dangers. 'They that will be rich fall into temptation and a snare, and into many foolish and hurtful lusts which drown men in destruction and perdition.'* So says the Apostle, and his teaching reminds us that there lies before a man of property an alternative—either personal consumption of his wealth or productive employment of it for the general social well-being. In the case of the 'rich fool' we see a man weighing these alternative schemes, 'What shall I do?'

* 1 Tim. vi. 9.

We have considered his choice and its fatal issue, and we may remember that it is the wrong choice in this matter that leads to the social consequences which seem to many so desperate, which produces 'Irreconcilables,' which suggests violent measures in relation to property, forcible readjustment of burdens, redress of intolerable wrongs, sweeping changes in the very framework of society.

Here, then, are Christian principles as to acquisition: (1) wealth *not* the true end of man; (2) property to be acquired justly; (3) to be acquired within the limits of moderation.

II. Passing now to the ethics of *use*, we are at least free from any uncertainty as to the teaching of our Lord. The Christian stands in a threefold relation to God, to his neighbour, to himself. He therefore owes duties in a threefold direction, and property is to be used under the restraints which these relationships impose. Wealth is to be employed in ways that are godly, righteous, and sober. Let us begin with the last first.

1. In relation to self—in regard to the personal use of wealth, the Christian law teaches *Sobriety, Temperance.* I would ask you to consider the truth of a statement in Mr. Charles Booth's work on 'Life and Labour in London.' He remarks that in the bright and busy life of London as we see it in crowded thoroughfares, 'men come and go, and are divorced from the sense of responsibility.' Consequently, 'extravagance, which is the exception in the life of each individual, becomes the rule.' We need to remember this significant warning against irresponsible extravagance and luxury, with its various evils, which, says a recent writer, 'nothing will remedy but an effectual attention to the idea of life as a whole, and a consideration whether its best purposes are being helped or hindered by our arrangements.'* Here is the very heart of the matter of personal expenditure. ' What is the purpose of my life, and how will my work be best promoted? What are the virtues I most need? How far

* Bosanquet, 'Civilization of Christendom,' p. 290.

will my expenditure develop in me industry, self-control, independence of mind?' The answer to these questions will obviously vary in different cases. The 'living wage' of a man will depend on the nature of his work; on the claims to which he is subject. There are in fact, as Professor Marshall has pointed out,* certain conventional necessaries which are required for personal efficiency; the skilled labourer differs from the unskilled; the professional man—the brain-worker—differs from the manual labourer. His necessaries, strictly so-called, are very numerous: 'the consumption of them is production; to abstain from consuming them is wasteful.' And yet, when all is said and done, 'more than half of the consumption of the upper classes of society in England is wholly unnecessary.'†

In relation, then, to personal expenditure, we must remember the law of Sobriety. The true end of our being is harmonious development of our faculties as moral and spiritual beings. Wealth is to be soberly enjoyed. 'He,' says Plato, 'who knows the temperate life will describe it as in all things gentle, having gentle pains and gentle pleasures and placid desires, and loves not insane.'‡ We must have a just sense of what self-development claims, and aim at not exceeding the limit that true sobriety allows.

2. Next, in relation to others, the great rule for property is *moral trusteeship*. This principle has been admirably stated in Mr. Lilly's book 'Right and Wrong': 'The only things which a man can in strictness call his own—and even here he is under the law of conscience—are his spiritual, intellectual, and physical faculties. The material object on which he exercises these faculties is subject to a higher ownership than his; to the indefeasible title of the human race represented to him by the community in which he lives. Of the material surroundings which he calls *mine*, he is but

---

* 'Principles of Economics,' vol. i., chap. iv.
† *Ibid.*, p. 124.
‡ 'Laws,' book v., 134.

a usufructuary, a trustee. The ultimate and inalienable ownership of what Aristotle called "the bounty of nature" is in the human race. Each country belongs, in the last resort, to its inhabitants in general; each country, with all that makes it a country—not merely its land, but all that has been taken from the land from time immemorial, and transformed into the various instruments of civilized life. . . . Not only the soil of the country, but its entire accumulated wealth, natural and fabricated, is, in the last resort, the property of the country.'* Such is the teaching of economic science, and Christianity supplements it by the rule that 'none of us liveth to himself.'† A man owes to the community the right use of his wealth. The true Christian thought of trusteeship replaces the old conventional conception (derived from Roman law) of irresponsible 'rights of property.' It is needless to remind you how vast a field lies open for private enterprise in mitigating, by wise outlay and well-considered employment of capital, the terrible inequalities of our social state. I need not enlarge on the miseries and the contrasts which were eloquently described to you last week.‡ If we try to find the root of the evils which perplex us, we shall find that St. Paul gives us a clue. 'In the last days perilous times—hard times§—shall come; for men shall be lovers of their own selves, lovers of money.' The source of our troubles is forgetfulness of the Christian law of trusteeship. Each man's conscience must be his guide as to the best direction in which he may render social service. The housing of the toiling poor; the promotion of education; the founding of schools and libraries; the care of the aged poor; the providing of recreation for the people; the building of refuges and labour homes; the formation of companies to promote co-operative enterprise,—these are some of the fields in which surplus wealth might reap a harvest; in which restitution might be made for past

---

* 'Right and Wrong,' pp. 197, 198.   † Rom. xiv. 7.
‡ By Archdeacon Farrar.   § 2 Tim. iii. 1, καιροὶ χαλεποί.

neglect; in which the grand truth of trusteeship might be practically acknowledged.

3. Lastly, beyond the personal needs that must be efficiently met—beyond the righteous claims of our fellow-men—there are the claims of Almighty God. It was the sin of the rich fool that he was not 'rich toward God.' It is true that in serving society—in ministering to those who in any sense are poor and in need—we are giving to God. His providence guides us to proper objects of beneficence. We owe a primary duty to our own kindred, our neighbourhood, our *employés*, our servants. But there are claims of God independent of the obligations which, when fulfilled towards His children and little ones, He accepts as rendered to Himself. Property owes a duty to Him as the Giver of all. The right of property is derived from Him; all that we have or enjoy is His gift. He is the ultimate lord of the soil.* He gives power to get wealth. So in relation to God the owner of property has to bear in mind the law of *accountability*. You will remember how vividly this truth is suggested by the parable of the steward who had wasted his master's goods, and who endeavoured by ingenuity to satisfy the just claims of his lord. At least the unjust steward recognised his accountability, which the rich fool did not; and we are to learn from the parable that the glory of God and the interests of His kingdom stand for us men even higher than the good of men. 'Thy kingdom come' stands before 'Thy will be done on earth.' Thus the claims of *religion* rise into prominence. There are works distinctively religious as well as social. For example, the care of the sick and dying and afflicted is a religious work (cf. St. Matt. xxv. 35 f.). Hospitals, homes for incurables, etc., owe their origin to the Christian spirit, and few services are more Christ-like than the founding of dispensaries and convalescent homes, or the endowment of parish nurses to visit and tend the poor in their own homes. Then there are great and crying needs to

* Wycliff, 'De dominio divino,' i. 8.

be met in the mission-field, at home and abroad; nay, great deeds of restitution to barbarous races, degraded by contact with the polluting vices of our civilization. There is urgent need of churches—great need of endowments for spiritual purposes, religious education, and the like. It is the great danger of an age of large and widespread wealth and luxury that it loses the sense of spiritual realities. That is why St. Paul* charges the rich to put their trust in the *living God;* not in the dead idol of riches, but in the God who is eternally alive, ever at work in the world, ever searching the deeds of men, ever bringing nearer the revelation of His kingdom. Happy those men of wealth who are conspicuous in devotion to God: like David, preparing for the building of the temple; like Zacchæus, hastening to entertain his Saviour; like Joseph and Nicodemus, providing costly interment for the sacred body of the Redeemer. Surely of all blessings that wealth can command, none, if we judge aright, is comparable to these.

We have dealt imperfectly with a very large subject. It seems fitting in these closing sermons of the series preached in this church to end by suggesting a thought peculiarly appropriate at this season. On the eve of the Holy Week let us remember what is the one fundamental remedy for our social evils—self-sacrifice. Self-sacrifice need not take precisely the form it took in the first days of the Church's history, when 'no man said that aught of the things which he possessed was his own, but they had all things common.' But it should be inspired by the same motive; it should be modelled after the same pattern, viz., the self-oblation of the Saviour Himself. What Frederick Robertson says is true, 'To the spirit of the Cross alone we look as the remedy for social evils. When the people of this country, especially the rich, shall have been touched with the spirit of the Cross to a largeness of sacrifice of which they have not dreamed as yet, there will be an atonement between the rights of labour

* 1 Tim. vi. 17.

and the rights of property.'* The solution of our problems is to be found in the Gospel of Jesus Christ. As we look around for remedies and aids we shall find none except in Him. 'Lord, to whom shall we go? Thou—Thou only, hast the words of eternal life.'

Note A.   (See Sermon I.)

Extract from a letter by Bishop Butler, in Fitzgerald's edition of the 'Analogy,' Preface, p. xciii:

'Property in general is, and must be, regulated by the laws of the community. This in general is, I say, allowed on all hands. If, therefore, there be any sort of property exempt from these regulations, or any exception to the general method of regulating it, such exception must appear, either from the light of nature or from revelation. But neither of these do, I think, show any such exception; and therefore we may with a good conscience retain any possession, church lands or tithes, which the laws of the State we live under give us property in. And there seems less ground for scruple here in England than in some other countries; because our ecclesiastical laws agree with our civil ones in the matter. Under the Mosaic dispensation, indeed, God Himself assigned to the priests and Levites tithes and other possessions; and in these possessions they had a Divine right, a property quite superior to all human laws, ecclesiastical as well as civil. But every donation to the Christian Church is a human donation, and no more; and therefore cannot give a Divine right, but such a right only as must be subject in common with all other property to the regulation of human laws. I would not carry you into abstruse speculation, but think it might be clearly shown that no one can have a right of perpetuity in any land except it be given by God, as the land of Canaan was to Abraham. There is no other means by which such a kind of property or right can be acquired, and plain absurdities would follow from the supposition of it. The persons, then, who gave these lands to the Church had themselves no right of perpetuity in them, consequently could convey no such right to the Church. But all scruples concerning the lawfulness of laymen possessing these lands go upon supposition that the Church has such a right of perpetuity in them; and therefore all these scruples must be groundless, as going upon a false supposition.'

---

* 'Sermons,' series i., p. 261.

COMMERCIAL MORALITY.*

BY THE

REV. J. CARTER,

OF PUSEY HOUSE, GENERAL SEC. C.S.U.

I.

'*Wherefore putting away lying, speak every man truth with his neighbour: for we are members one of another.*'—EPHESIANS iv. 25.

WHY speak of 'commercial morality'? Surely for the Christian there is but one moral standard, even our Lord's command, 'Be ye perfect.' It recognises no exceptions, it is meant to control every department of social life. Why, then, not leave professional men to apply their Christian principles for themselves? For two reasons chiefly. Firstly, because a good many 'practical' men have assumed that Christian principles have nothing to do with 'business,' and that commerce is mechanically regulated by its own peculiar 'laws.' Thus prices are fixed by the law of supply and demand. When buyer and seller transact business, they enter into a 'free contract,' the terms of which are settled by the higgling of the market. And to obviate any further doubt in the matter, you may appeal to the principle of *caveat emptor!* If people are fools enough to pay for articles of fashion a hundred per cent. more than they are worth, or if they allow themselves

* Of the two following sermons neither was written out before delivery, and both are given here in a much shortened form.

to be deceived by shoddy or adulterated goods, you have a 'right' to make a profit out of their foolishness. Such a view of business may be condemned absolutely. It finds no sort of reasonable justification either in political economy or in physical science, and obviously it cannot be maintained by a true Christian. And, secondly, because many professed Christians are tempted to great moral laxity in regard to their business conduct. While hating some of these 'laws' and trade customs, they have more or less conformed to them under the increasing stress of competition. It is to this class especially that the Christian preacher can make his appeal. He is not called upon to be the keeper of other men's consciences, nor to relieve practical men of any part of their personal responsibility. His main duty is simply to put pressure on the Christian conscience of practical men, to stimulate its more vigorous action, and to claim a fuller realization of fundamental principles which are the common property of all true believers. Therefore, all I can with authority demand from you is a renewal of your faith and confidence in those elementary principles of Christian morality which we learned in the homely words of the Church Catechism about our duty to our neighbour. And if beyond this I venture to make any practical suggestions, they must be judged by you on their merits.

It will be convenient to divide the subject into two parts: (i.) The actual conditions before us. (ii.) The remedies to be proposed.

(i.) There can be no doubt that the prevailing methods of business are utterly deplorable from the moral point of view. Some time ago the Oxford branch of the Christian Social Union sent out a number of questions on 'Commercial Morality' to practical men, and the answers received go far to justify the deliberate opinion of Mr. Herbert Spencer on this subject:

'It has been said that the law of the animal creation is: "Eat and be eaten"; and of our trading community it may be similarly said that its law is, "Cheat and be cheated." A system of keen competition, carried on, as it is, without adequate moral restraint, is very much a system of commercial cannibalism. Its alternatives are, "Use the same weapons as your antagonist, or be conquered and devoured."*

Let me quote a few of the replies to the question, 'Do you find it difficult to apply the principles of Christian truth and justice to the conduct of business?'

Two employers write:

'Business is based on the gladiatorial theory of existence. If Christian truth and justice is not consistent with this, business is in a bad case. So is nature.'

'You take it evidently for granted that such things are unjustifiable from the moral standpoint, so that, of course, the only excuses one can make are that everyone does it, and that one must live. In my own business I have not much trouble of this kind, and what I have I generally weakly give in to.' And then, in regard to a particular piece of roguery sometimes practised, he remarks, 'I have never done this with my *own hand*, though my clerk does it. I do not like it, and hardly know what I should do if asked to do it *myself!* As it is, I leave it to their own consciences, feeling I must live somehow, and knowing I cannot afford to lose a good customer.'

And a commercial traveller and a draper's assistant reply as follows:

'Not only difficult, but impossible. For a man is not master of himself. If one would live, and avoid the bankruptcy court, one must do business on the same lines as others do, without troubling whether the methods are in harmony with the principles of Christian truth and justice or not.'

'Extremely so. The tendency to misrepresent, deceive, or take unfair advantage under circumstances that

* 'The Morals of Trade.'

daily offer the opportunity of so doing, is generally too strong to resist where self-interest is the motive power of action, the conventional morality the only check. To me they appear to be opposing principles—the first of self-sacrifice, the second of self-interest.'

Of course there are well-established firms who can afford to lose business rather than use dishonest methods; but, from all accounts, it is evident that honourable trade is very considerably hampered by unjust competition.

'If it were possible,' one writes, 'to do away with competition, the excuse and justification for a large proportion of commercial immorality would be gone. There would then be a chance for a man to trade honestly with a reasonable prospect of success. I believe there are thousands of Christian business men who would be glad of this chance. They would then have a free hand, unhampered by the system of unjust, not to say dishonest, competition.'*

(ii.) What, then, is to be done? We know from history the method of Christianity in dealing with existing institutions and customs, *e.g.*, slavery. It first makes them, at least, tolerable, and then proceeds either to transform or to abolish them. So, now, in regard to the prevailing system of trade competition, it would at once assume a quite different complexion if only there were a more general recognition of the simple duty of truthfulness. And surely this much may be claimed dogmatically! The Christian appeal is, in the first instance, to the individual man of business, and it says, *Be honest yourself!* Is this too heroic? Is it too much to expect that the merchant should be as chivalrous as the soldier? Certainly it will cost a man something to be a Christian, for there is no reason to suppose that the days of martyrdom are wholly past and gone. However, 'it is required in stewards, that a man be found faithful.'†

---

* A large number of the replies received from business men to the above questions have been published in a pamphlet entitled 'Commercial Morality' (Rivington, Percival and Co.).

† 1 Cor. iv. 2.

To illustrate my meaning, I may mention three details, three practices which appear to be absolutely wrong, the removal of which would mean an enormous change in commercial life : (1) Adulteration of goods which cannot reasonably be expected to be known to the buyer. (2) False or misleading statements as to the quality or history of goods. (3) Commissions to employés (as distinct from fees to commission agents or brokers) when given as bribes for breaches of trust. It would be easy to give definite instances of all these immoral methods of transacting business, but, as practical men, you will be able to supply these facts for yourselves.

In the next place, I would urge *organization for mutual support*. If we could discover the standard which the best business men set before themselves, and form a strong association for its maintenance, much might be accomplished towards the elimination of unjust and dishonourable competition. Something has already been done in this direction by the Chambers of Commerce, but there is need of an educated and vigorous Christian public opinion over a wider area. Perhaps I may add that one practical result of some private conferences recently held between members of the Christian Social Union and some prominent business men will probably be the formation of a 'Fair-dealing League,' and I should be glad to hear from anyone who would be willing to help in such work.

So, then, I have nothing new to offer, no 'Morrison's pill' to obviate all further business anxieties, but simply the old Christian warning, 'Putting away lying, speak every man truth with his neighbour.' Oh, the shame of it! That it should be necessary in London to urge this as a fitting lesson for Lent. Why all this chicanery? Are we becoming poorer? Is nature more niggardly? Is God less bountiful? People prate about the decline of agriculture; the ruin of our foreign trade; the depreciation of silver; the lack of employment for willing workers, and the hard times generally.

But what are the facts? Distress there is certainly—terrible, shameful distress in various parts of society—but it is mainly due, as I believe, to our mismanagement of God's bounty, our wastefulness, our abominable selfishness. The wealth of England has been increasing at a much greater rate than the population; and at the present time we are far more competent to support every man, woman, and child in existence than at any previous period in the history of the country.

Surely, then, we can afford to try some experiments. And all I ask now is, that we should try the experiment of honesty. Truth-telling has been a characteristic of the English race, and the splendid fabric of England's commercial and industrial supremacy is still a proof that in the long-run 'Honesty is the best policy.' But now we are more than ever tempted to fall away from the high standard of business integrity; and the pressure that is upon us is not so much the pressure of foreign competition as of that nearer home. What we have to fear most is the reckless competition of English capital, English brains and English brawn, especially when uncontrolled by any moral principles. And if only this trade competition could be restrained within something like reasonable limits, if only the game could be played fairly with some regard for simple truth and common honesty, the existing system would appear much more tolerable. If only we could dare to be honest, it would bring steadiness to trade, it would take the keen edge off this frantic struggle for wealth, and it would tend to make us more like what I pray God we all would wish to be—true men and loyal brothers in Jesus Christ.

COMMERCIAL MORALITY.

BY THE

REV. J. CARTER.

II.

'Therefore all things whatsoever ye would that men should do to you, do ye even so to them.'—MATTHEW vii. 12.

I WAS speaking yesterday of the claims of honesty; to-day I have to deal with the claims of brotherhood. It is my duty to endeavour to emphasize the great fact that Christian morality can never be satisfied with merely preventing the most obvious forms of deceit and dishonesty, but must go on to fulfil the whole law of Christ. What, then, is the work that lies before us?

First of all, I will mention, as briefly as possible, the Christian method of trade and commerce; secondly, I will offer a few practical suggestions for your consideration and judgment; and, thirdly, I should like to say a few words by way of encouragement.

I. What is the Christian method of business? The main object that we have to set before us is to substitute the principle of co-operation for that of competition, or the principle of socialism for that of individualism. You will please observe that I am speaking of principles, I am not now concerned with this or that system. The principle of individualism is wholly unchristian and utterly discredited; it is unchristian in that it appeals to self-interest, and it is discredited because it is based upon two absurd fallacies. It assumes that every man knows what is for his own true interest and will follow it; and again, that out of the clashing of private interests the common welfare will result. Both these assumptions are disproved by an appeal to history. We have, therefore, nothing left but the moral principle of co-operation, which is at the root of all that is good in socialism, and which bids us take as our common aim the fulfilment of brotherly service.

For instance, let us consider from this point of view the relation between buyer and seller. They have no right whatsoever to try to overreach one another. On the contrary, if they are two Christian men, they should bring in the principle of reciprocity, and their positions should be interchangeable. The seller should not ask a higher price for an article he wishes to sell than what he, knowing the circumstances, would give if he were in the buyer's position. On the other hand, the buyer should not endeavour to beat down the price which the seller asks, by taking any unfair advantage over him. The transaction should not be a 'bargain' in the ordinary sense of a loss to one of the parties concerned, but rather a fair exchange of mutual benefit.

II. How are we to set about realizing our ideal? In trying to explain how this may be done, let me speak, first, of the duty of the purchaser; next, of the duty of the seller; and, thirdly, of the duty of society. (*a*) What is the duty of the purchaser? Here we touch a question which concerns everybody. The more one looks into the present industrial conditions, the more one realizes the tremendous responsibility that lies upon the ordinary consumer. We find that the general public are more or less devoured by a passion for cheapness. We must insist, therefore, upon the duty of every individual not to be satisfied by merely paying a price which those who sell an article are willing to take. The purchaser should, if possible, go behind that, and discover the conditions under which wares offered for sale have been produced.

Here we are met with two objections. The first is, How can I afford to do this? After a lecture in Bethnal Green some time ago on this subject, a man stood up and asked, 'How can I afford to do what you say? I must go to the cheapest place I can find.' 'If you are a Christian man,' was the reply, 'and the shirts you have on your back mean the misery and degradation of your sisters, you should sooner go without than wear them!' And he could understand the principle when it was explained to him, for he had just been on strike. He had dared to subject his wife and children to the risk of starvation. Why did he not rather take a lower wage? For the sake of his family, of his class, and of generations to come he was willing to jeopardize his own life and the welfare of his family. And he was right, and he must be prepared to do the same thing again should similar circumstances arise.

The second objection is the difficulty of obtaining information about trade conditions. But if we can induce a sufficient number of the general public to have a conscience on the subject, and to be willing to act up to their conscience, then I am quite sure that practical men will be only too ready to supply adequate information. We have had some little experience of this in Oxford, where such information has been provided in response to a demand for the facts. Moreover, these remarks apply to that large class of people who receive interest for capital invested in some particular company or business, and who are to some extent responsible for the conditions under which it is carried on. It has been said in some quarters that this would put a very serious and grievous burden upon the Christian conscience. But as shareholders do not find it difficult to give attention to their dividends in the case of fraud or mismanagement, so they should consider also the conditions of the company's employés, whence their profit is derived. For instance, a few weeks ago I had a letter from a shareholder in a certain railway company, asking if he should give up his shares, because the company was treating its employés in a way he could not justify. The answer in this case was, of course, 'No; your responsibility is limited; you are only responsible for your vote and influence. Stay where you are, and, when the opportunity occurs, use your vote and influence for securing better terms for the workmen.'

(*b*) What is the duty of the seller? Here again time will only allow me to deal with two or three salient points, which I will endeavour to define by way of negatives. For example, there are three sins against the law of brotherhood which are not uncommonly committed by business men. It seems impossible to justify a merchant in selling at absolutely less than cost price in order to injure his competitors, excepting only in a few special cases in which this practice may be legitimate, as, for instance, when there is some great fluctuation in the market, or when the seller is compelled to do so in self-defence by unjust competition. Again, it is hardly moral for either a trading company or an individual capitalist already established in trade to undersell competitors with an idea in the long-run of getting a monopoly, and then raising prices. Further, there is that large field of speculation in 'futures' and 'options,' which seems to me to be nothing short of gambling of the worst kind. In fact, the results of this system are so disastrous that an 'Anti-option Bill' has been proposed in America, simply to make it illegal for a man to sell what he has not got. All this artificial buying and selling of things which do not exist is bound in the long-run to oppress the real producer, and really means robbing other people of their property.*

(*c*) What is the duty of society? First of all, we have to conceive the idea which mediæval Churchmen expressed in

* Cf. 'Commercial Gambling,' by C. W. Smith.

the term *justum pretium*. Goods offered for sale should be sold at a fair price; and this implies an adequate wage for the producer which will provide him with the means of living a decent life both morally and materially. Then we have to consider how far it is possible to maintain, or even to raise our standards, through the power of association for a common end. It is true, comparing modern with mediæval conditions, that our theory of value is much more subjective than was theirs, and that the various grades of society were much more clearly defined in the Middle Ages than now. But at least we can keep before our minds the great principle that under given conditions every article has a fair and just price. This principle is by no means an innovation; it has been struggling for recognition all along. And we can mark our advance in this direction by observing, as we travel eastwards, that business is more and more settled by the mere 'higgling of the market.' Moreover, we have in England taken a notable step towards the determination of price during the last few months. The recent crisis in the coal trade has brought prominently forward the need of some limit to the practice of 'cutting' rates, which has found expression in the popular phrase, 'a living wage.' The phrase is ambiguous, and is obviously open to abuse; it would perhaps be better to speak of 'a standard wage,' which may be raised, and which possibly may have to fall. But at all events we require some standard to act as a barrier against unregulated and unscrupulous competition. And to secure this, and to maintain fair and honourable conditions of trade, it is evident that we cannot trust to individual employers, or to individual workmen, or to this or that class by itself. What we want is a strong and well-disciplined organization of the masters, and an equally strict and comprehensive organization of the men; we want to see these rival associations uniting together on a board of conciliation, made up of an equal number of members from either side, for the purpose of satisfactory settlement of trade disputes.

If this is not sufficient at a crisis, we must have some supervision or control on the part of the State as representing the whole community, or the active influence of an organization of consumers resolute to support the best of the masters and of the men in securing just conditions. If we do not get this organization in a rational and Christian way, it will come in an irrational and unchristian way. We have only to look across the Atlantic, where individualism has had free play, to see how the commerce of that great country is controlled by gigantic combinations owned by a very small section of the community; which state of things a good many men in America feel is wholly against the best interests of the country.

III. I have been forced to speak very rapidly, so that I might at least touch upon a few of the main points, all of which bristle with difficulties. But I fully realize how complex these problems are, and how exceeding slow our progress will be. Therefore, it may be as well for me to speak a word of encouragement by reminding you of the fact that I am not making an appeal which has never been made to Christian men before, nor asking the Church to do what the Church has not done again and again. For instance, in Italy, at the end of the eleventh century, a great development of trade was going on, and in order to explain the new conditions that arose, it was necessary to develop a new jurisprudence. From the Roman law, two theories were extracted which were used to justify the ordinary customs of business men. One was the theory of the absolute right of private property in the unchristian sense that a man has a right to do what he likes with his own. The other was the recognition of an unlimited freedom of contract apart from any previous moral considerations. In this way they endeavoured to justify the ordinary course of trade, and I need not tell you that a society based on two such principles is sure to come to grief. In order to cope with these evil tendencies, Churchmen began a fresh consideration of economic questions. They studied the facts, they applied their Christian principles, and formulated rules for the guidance of conduct. They made their appeal to the individual conscience, and with such good effect that finally practical men in their various secular organizations were moved to regulate these matters more in accordance with Christian morality.* And now once more this appears to be just the sort of work that earnest Christians are called upon to perform. The professors of political economy are quite clear about their own special work. They say, 'We merely state facts. The existing methods of trade may be moral or immoral; the results good or bad. We leave it to men of conscience and common-sense to decide what Christian men of business ought to do.' And though the task is not an easy one and the difficulties are considerable, there is at the same time every reason to be encouraged. Whichever way we turn there is opportunity for us to do something deliberately, systematically, and unitedly, in the directions indicated.

Let me briefly conclude with two quotations. On the one hand, in regard to the responsibility of society as a whole, we have Professor Marshall writing that 'Public opinion, based on sound economics and just morality, will, it may be hoped, become ever more and more the arbiter of the conditions of industry.'† And, on the other hand, with a view to encouraging our hopefulness, we have been recently reassured by the Bishop of Durham that 'There is about us enough spiritual force and action to win the world,' but, alas! it is so 'dispersed, undisciplined, undirected.'‡ Therefore the duty that lies upon us now is to summon the forces at our command, and to concentrate our energies. Above all let us understand that the grace of God does not fail as it comes down through the ages. His power is still with us,

---

* Cf. Ashley's 'Economic History,' book i., chap. iii.
† 'Economics of Industry,' p. 411.
‡ 'The Incarnation and Common Life,' p. 14.

and is as strong as ever to inspire and brace the human will. The claim our Lord makes upon business men to-day is the same as that which He laid upon His first followers. It is expressed in the principle which mediæval theologians applied so successfully to the economic problems of their own generation. And it should be the regulative test of the Christian conduct of trade and commerce now, 'All things whatsoever ye would that men should do to you, do ye even so to them.'

WAGES.

BY THE

REV. WILLIAM CUNNINGHAM, D.D.,

FELLOW OF TRINITY COLLEGE, CAMBRIDGE; AND PROFESSOR OF POLITICAL ECONOMY, KING'S COLLEGE, LONDON.

'The labourer is worthy of his hire.'—ST. LUKE x. 10.

THERE are different ways in which our religion may come to influence our conduct towards our neighbours. It may sometimes point out kindnesses that we ought to do, from love to God, towards our fellow-creatures—virtues which we might not feel bound to cultivate at all, if it were not for the teaching and example of our Lord; and sometimes our Christian belief serves, not to point out new duties, but to give us better reasons and stronger motives for doing the ordinary moral duties, which good men of any creed and any time have recognised as binding upon them. It is well, I think, that we should try to keep these two distinct in our minds, to see, at least, how far ordinary morality will carry us—the morality of the man who makes no profession of religion—before we go on to consider what is specifically Christian.

This distinction is drawn for us pointedly by the old-fashioned proverb which bids us be *just* before we are *generous*. In thinking about duty in regard to wages, we have to do primarily with what is *just*, not so much with what is *generous* or *philanthropic* or *charitable*. The labourer *is worthy of his hire.* We have to try ourselves by considerations of *justice*, and not, in the first instance, at any rate, by any sentiment of kindliness or self-sacrifice or brotherly love. These have their place, too, as we shall presently see; but the fundamental ethical question is not one of pity for the poor or help for the needy, but of *justice* between man and man, justice to be done all the more carefully and eagerly by the professing Christian, but still justice as recognised and understood by all.

I. The accusation of injustice in our existing social arrangements is frequently uttered and readily repeated. We continually hear that the labourer *ought* 'to have a larger share of the wealth which his labour creates.' Viewed as a simple question of justice, it seems a very difficult one to pronounce upon. If, as some ignorant* people think—and the language of Adam Smith gives at least some apparent economic authority for their opinion—manual labour, alone and unassisted, were the sole factor in the production of wealth, there would be little more to be said from the point of view of justice; but, though a necessary element, labour is not by any means the only necessary element. Our whole industrial organization is very complicated; the manual labourer has not either the *means* or the *opportunity* of labouring by himself and on his own account. The *capitalist*, who may often be a sleeping partner, supplies the *means*—materials, and tools; the *employer*, who manages the business, and who may be either a capitalist, or the agent of the capitalists, takes orders and hires men; he supplies *opportunity* of working. It is possible that some better method of supplying the manual worker with the means of labour and the opportunity of labour may be found, though personally I have little ex-

---

* This phrase does not, so far as I see, and certainly was not meant to, apply to scientific socialists who would reconstitute society altogether, but to persons I have met who accept the present constitution of society, and yet advocate changes which are incompatible with its continued existence.

pectation of any very immediate or substantial alteration in this respect. But the question is whether, under these existing conditions of industry, the reward of labour is just. And this question involves many problems of great difficulty.

1. (*a*) In the first place, it is not easy for any outsider like myself to know what the division is, at the present time, in any trade. Partly owing to the credit system, and partly owing to other circumstances, there is a decided, and possibly a necessary, reticence on the part of employers and capitalists as to the profits of business. Even in those cases of joint-stock concerns, where the accounts are printed and sent to the shareholders, it is not usual to give such details as enable the outsider to judge what the division really is. This reticence seems to me very much to be regretted; there may, of course, be good and sufficient reasons for it of which I am unaware, but it serves to engender the suspicion that profits and salaries are unduly large, and that suspicion is likely to continue and grow so long as the concealment is maintained.

(*b*) Another difficulty is this—the functions performed by the manual labourer, the capitalist, and the employer, are all necessary, but they are very different; it is extremely difficult to compare them with one another, or to say at what ratio they ought to be respectively rewarded. The disagreeables of the labourer's lot are obvious—hard physical toil, with risk of accident to life and limb, and very insecure tenure of his employment; generosity or charity may well take these into account, but mere justice has rather to consider the importance of his personal contribution to the total result, as compared with the importance of the personal contributions of others; each element is necessary, but some are more difficult to procure than others—just as air and food are alike necessary for life, but food is harder to secure than air; and justice must take this kind of consideration into account. It has to weigh against one another according to their respective importance, and therefore their fair reward—the *physical work* of the labourer, the *mental work* of the employer, and the *enterprise* of the capitalist in undertaking the pecuniary risks of business. It seems to me very hard to say how such incommensurable elements should be rewarded respectively; but perhaps I may point out, in passing, that if one looks back over a century or two it is clear that the rate of the reward of enterprise is steadily declining; also that, with the invention of machinery, manual skill is no longer of such predominant importance in production as it once was, while the skill and organizing faculties of the employer are far more taxed than was ever the case before; business capacity is the one of the three necessary elements which now seems to be of increased importance, and to receive a greatly increased rate of reward.

(*c*) All such calculations are, however, beset by a third difficulty; where, as in a very large proportion of businesses, the employer works with his own capital, it is impossible for outsiders, and it may be difficult for him, to assess the reward he draws as employer (for wages of management), and the reward he gets as capitalist for the money invested in the business. Again, as the labourer always gets paid something, while the capitalist sometimes makes losses, and sometimes gets large gains, it is very difficult to compare the actual remuneration, on the whole, of those who reap their reward in such different forms.

Under these circumstances, it seems as if it were hardly possible to take such obscure and complicated considerations into account, and to get at the justice of the case. There is, however, one way in which we may, I think, cut the knot; we may find a rough-and-ready test of justice, or rather, perhaps, of injustice, by looking at *expediency*. We may frame this canon, *that what is expedient for any business as a whole, is not obviously unjust for any of the partners in that business*. It is expedient for any business, on the whole, that each of the three necessary factors should be adequately supplied and maintained; it is expedient that capital should be so rewarded that there may be money available for the development and expansion of business; it is expedient that business capacity should be so rewarded that men of energy and enterprise should be willing to devote themselves to the management of its affairs; it is well that labour should be so rewarded that the workman may be vigorous in mind and body, and thoroughly at his best. And, tried by this test, it may at least be doubted if the two elements which are largely rewarded are over-rewarded, or get more than what is expedient. It is at least arguable that the present prospects of the reward of capital are such, that it is not readily forthcoming for the farther development of railway enterprise. It is obvious that the high salaries paid for business capacity in that line of life are paid to men who have worked their way up, and proved themselves to be worth the money. Tried by this test, it is hard to say that either the capitalist or the employer gets *too much*, or has an unjustly large share.

2. But even if this be true, there seem to be grounds for urging that the labourer gets *too little;* it seems as if the employer and the capitalist, with their requirements, were first taken account of, and the labourer had to be satisfied with the leavings. To some extent this has been, to some extent it is, true. We must therefore fall back on those farther questions, How far is it true that the labourer gets too little? What test can we apply to see whether the labourer is unjustly treated and does not get enough?

And, so far as I see, the best test we can apply is a physical one; the labourer gets enough if he has the material means of being at his best; kept in good health, vigorous, and alert in mind and body, and able to maintain a home in which he can rear vigorous, intelligent, and moral children to succeed him in time. *Efficiency* present and to come is the test of *sufficiency*. If the labourer is so fed and clothed that he cannot work vigorously; if he is overstrained, so that he becomes prematurely old; if his children are decrepit and miserably fed, so that they never grow up to be fit for hard and regular work—then, assuredly, he has too little. On the causes and possible cure I may have more to say; but at the moment let me add that I think the verdict of the casual observer in this country at present would be, that some labourers are paid sufficiently to enable them and their children to be efficient, and that some are not. Let us think a little of each in turn.

(*a*) For those who in the present day enjoy a 'sufficiency of wages,' those who are sometimes spoken of as the aristocracy of labour, there is one thing worth remembering. We are still viewing it all as a question of justice—mere justice. *The labourer is worthy of his hire.* Yes, he ought to be; but is he? Is every man's work worth the money that is paid him? If he gets sufficient wage, does he do efficient labour for it? There are many complaints rife of men who are incompetent, of men who shirk and scamp, who idle, out of an ignorant desire to make work for the unemployed. For the apostolic maxim, 'That if any would not work, neither should he eat,' has a double bearing: it does pronounce a condemnation on those who, relieved from the task of providing for personal needs, do not set themselves to do service in some fashion to God and man, but live in laziness. But it also condemns those who, taking the wages of labour, yet idle away their time. Assuredly, if justice demands that the labourer should get a sufficient wage, it insists, not less imperatively, that he shall do the work for which he is paid efficiently and well.

(*b*) For here, at least, justice and expediency coincide; we may all welcome every possible step in progress, every raising of the standard of comfort of the working man in every branch of industry. But for those classes of labour which have sufficient at present, there is only one way in which a farther improvement can come by *increased efficiency*. If there is a larger net result of the combined energy of employers and employed, there will be more for each; there is a possibility of an increased reward for labour which can be permanently maintained, because it is really earned. But an increased reward, which neither arises from nor calls forth increased efficiency, is hardly likely to be maintained; it is likely to attract outsiders to migrate and compete for this highly-paid work, and there will be difficulty in excluding them. Or it may be secured at the expense of the capitalist and employers, or at the expense of the public; and in either case there is a danger of an injury to the trade which may react on the wage-earner. For instance, a limitation of hours, which *does not call forth more efficiency*, but merely distributes employment among more hands, and produces the same result at greater expense to capitalists or the public, is likely to injure the trade, and to afford, before many months elapse, less regular employment than before. For, indeed, the days of privilege have gone by; no class of workers can secure and maintain specially favourable conditions for itself, at the expense of the public and to the exclusion of other workers, unless it can prove its title by superior efficiency. An improved wage thus secured, thus justly won, is a real gain; but any attempt of those, whose wages are sufficient, to secure a larger reward without increased efficiency and at the expense either of the public or the employers, is of doubtful expediency; it does not seem to be a just demand.

(*c*) We have seen in what direction we must look for the improvement of the wages of those who have sufficient; we shall find that a very similar reason accounts for the starvation wages which too many others are compelled to take; their wages are *insufficient*, because they themselves are *inefficient;* they may be very laborious and industrious, but what they do is some trivial, mechanical work, quickly learned and easily done. And hence it seems that there is a sense in which starvation wages are not unjust—not unjust as between man and man; the work done is worth little, and as a mere matter of justice it cannot be highly paid. To insist that we ought to pay more than the market rate for work, is to appeal to the kindness of the charitable, but no such obligation is incumbent on any man out of mere justice.

3. This seems to be a hard doctrine, and there need be no surprise that many are at present inclined to urge that justice, in an extended sense, demands that all who labour hard and long shall be able to secure in return the necessaries and decencies of life. This is the feeling that lies at the bottom of much of the demand for a *living wage.** When this demand is made on behalf of the lowest and least well paid portion of the population, as if it were a duty for public authority to step in and ensure them a sufficiency by law, we are bound to scrutinize the proposal closely.

(*a*) A good deal of isolated evidence can be adduced in favour of this proposal; there can be no doubt that an attempt of this kind might, in some circumstances and in some trades, produce beneficial results. There are cases where people, if they were better paid, would be able to do better work, and the raising of their wages would be economically successful, since it would call forth more efficiency. I have often heard this alleged as proved by experience in certain classes of agricultural labour.

(*b*) Nor need we be deterred from the experiment by the fear that some trades would be killed off altogether. If they cannot be maintained in this country, except on terms which are permanently degrading to a section of the population, it is at least a question whether they should be maintained at all. There is no real kindness in inducing men to stick to a dying trade—as the handloom weavers stuck to their calling, and starved at it. The line taken by the

---

* 'The endeavour to fix a living wage from time to time in trades that have a sufficiency on the whole, so as to prevent the rate of reward falling below that level, seems to me to be quite on a different footing from any proposal to introduce a living wage as a means of elevating the sweated classes.'—*Contemporary Review*, January, 1894.

men who insisted on passing the great Factory Acts was that it would be better that the cotton trade should be destroyed than that it should continue under the then existing conditions. On this principle we may still take our stand.

(c) But still I can have no hope for the success of any attempt to raise the standard of comfort of the poorest classes by merely insisting that they shall be better paid. For, after all, to give a man more money is to give him an opportunity—there is no security that he will take advantage of it. The mere offering of opportunities does not in itself bring about improvement; if things were readjusted so that opportunities of rising were always available, this very fact might even engender greater carelessness about making the most of them. If we think of the past and of the present, we shall see how many existing opportunities of rising are misused; how some are inclined to take out any additional gain in mere idleness, and some in excess of one kind or another, and some in improvident marriage. I do not speak harshly of such human weakness, I note it as a fact—a fact that is familiar enough to everyone—for who among us is not aware that he has wasted some of his opportunities, and thrown away some of his chances by carelessness and folly? To provide the opportunity of improvement is much, but it is not enough; it certainly is not all that is needed; and when we see what a little way it would take us, how much disorganization it must cause, how much temptation it would offer, how little good it would ensure, we can only say that what is so little expedient cannot be really right.

II. Is there, then, no way out of the trouble, no hope before us? None that I see so long as we confine ourselves to the thought of justice, and the mere endeavour to carry this plain duty into effect. No simple appeal to mere justice will take us very far when we once see that there is a question of elevating a large section of the population to a better condition, material, intellectual, and moral. No cut-and-dry formula will solve the difficulty of really raising them. We must go to something else than justice; we must rely on a principle that is characteristically, if not exclusively, Christian—on charity or philanthropy. Justice does not demand that we should continue unweariedly to offer opportunities of improvement to those who may misuse them; but charity does, charity beareth all things, believeth all things, hopeth all things. It is not easily provoked, it is not easily discouraged—only such a principle as this can persist unweariedly in the task before us.

And if that task is to be accomplished, charity must be not only enthusiastic and hopeful, but wise; we must add knowledge to zeal. It is terrible to think how much mischief has been done and misery brought about by careless and ignorant kindness. The African slave trade to America is a monument of the evil that well-meaning philanthropy may do: it was introduced by a man who desired to relieve the American of arduous work for which he was unfitted, and to substitute a stronger race. The degraded pauperism of the beginning of this century was the direct result of the well-meaning philanthropy of magistrates who relaxed the stringency of poor-law administration in a time of temporary distress—a proved act of folly which some seem ready to repeat. Above all, let us remember this—justice may lay down and apply a general principle, but it cannot be so in the same way with charity, for charity cannot accomplish its task wholesale; it must be discriminating, and personal, and careful, if it is to find out the best way of giving the poorest and the most degraded a better chance, over and over again.

And if we thus turn to Christianity for the principle that can afford opportunity, we shall also find in it a power to call forth effort to use any new opportunity; there is help which is characteristically, if not exclusively, Christian on this side also. Here we can find an ideal of life, an ideal which we shall never outlive, for it is supernatural, and yet an ideal which floats but a little way before us, which is visualized and depicted in terms of earthly things—we look for a new and a better earth. And as our religion affords an ideal to kindle enthusiasm, so, too, it can, not less truly, supply the strength to struggle undauntedly on, to rise above hopelessness, to overcome passion, to shake off the evil that besets men and keeps them down. The miseries of the world reappear in new and changing forms, but the old remedies are at hand—more faith in the power of Christ, more hope for the triumph of Christ, more likeness to the loving nature of Christ. These we may rely on, and they cannot fail, for there is indeed a Name given whereby men may be saved from degradation, as from every other ev thing.

THE UNEMPLOYED.

BY THE

REV. CANON BARNETT,
WARDEN OF TOYNBEE HALL.

'And Nathan said to David, Thou art the man.'—2 SAMUEL xii. 7.

AN enchantment seems to lie on the land. Work is waiting to be done; workers are waiting to do the work; capital is waiting employment. Streets, for want of cleaning or repair, threaten the public health; and buildings, for want of decoration or variety, depress energy. Hands, which might clean away the dirt and make beauty, are unemployed; and capital, which might use the unemployed hands, lies idle. Work, workers, capital, are waiting. It seems, as in the old fairy tales, as if only a touch were wanting to break the enchantment and set capital on employing the workers to do the work. It seems as if one impulse might substitute the buzz of happy industry for the sullen silence of idleness. As in the fairy tales, there are many aspirants to give the touch which will break the enchantment. They come with their scheme or their nostrum, their ballot-box or their dynamite, and they claim that they are the saviours of society who will provide for the unemployed.

We are here to-day as Christians to consider this strange condition. We put ourselves, therefore, first of all, in the presence of Christ. We turn from the sight of the want and the waste; we give up being anxious and careful about many things, that we may sit for a moment at the feet of

Christ. Christian work must begin with Christian prayer. In Christ's presence there is peace. Our passion of humanity becomes no less, but our patience becomes greater. Our hearts are still on fire, but the fire is restrained. Fire which will not bear restraint will never burn ; and Paul, the most passionate of Apostles, preached, 'Let your moderation be known among all men.' Calm, therefore, from the presence of Christ we come back to consider the world in which we live, with its idle and unemployed, its waste and its want.

1. We see that modern society is not altogether bad and corrupt. Some of its members may be degraded by wealth or by poverty; some may suffer for want of work; but the majority of the people are occupants of happy homes. Excessive poverty is no more common than excessive wealth, and there is more of good-will than of ill-will among men. Unhappiness, like disease, is the exception ; happiness, like wealth, is the rule. A poet is wanted to tell of the life lived in the houses which demurely face London and suburban streets—the simple family life of hard work and fireside happiness—where the rare pleasure is a stimulant and not a drug, where love, cherished by daily contact, bears its burdens as a joy, and shows itself in kindly thoughts and gentle charities. There are few sweeter sights on earth than a workman's home, and there is a sort of blasphemy in the exaggerations which speak of universal wretchedness. Reformers may weep over London as Jesus wept over Jerusalem ; but they may go, as Jesus went, to simple homes where they may find rest and refreshment for body and mind, as they watch the housewife neatly busy, as they hear the children laugh, or spend the quiet evening-hour in reading or in talk.

2. While peace and calm still rule our vision, we see also that the unemployed are not what passion or pity pictures them. The vast majority are not capable, skilled men who have no work to do; and those who have no work are not

always those who want work. Inquiry shows that in trades unions making monthly returns only about seven per cent. of their members are out of work, for all causes, at the worst season of the year.

Inquiry further shows that many who register themselves as unemployed are unfit for work. They have not the strength, the physical and mental capacity, to meet modern requirements; or they have not the character—the self-restraint—to be punctual or sober. Where work has been offered, as at Leeds and Millbank, it has been found that ninety per cent. of the applicants have been of this casual class—men who by choice or incapacity have been unable to do continuous work.

Lastly, it is obvious that, among all classes of society, there are some men who will not work—confirmed loafers, who live on the carelessness of society or their families.

The unemployed, calmly considered, is not an army of willing workers; but is rather a body largely made up of those half employed, those unfit for employment, and those unwilling to be employed. As Mr. C. Booth has said, 'Lack of work is not really the disease, and the mere provision of it is therefore useless as a cure.' There is, doubtless, a minority ready for regular work and unable to find it; but these do not make the mass whose numbers overwhelm thought.

Those reformers are wrong who would upset society, and destroy the happy homes of the many, in the hope of finding work for the unemployed.

The patience of our Lord's Passion—His dignity, His restraint, His calm—makes it impossible for His followers to be mere revolutionists or railing accusers of the ignorant and selfish. 'He that believeth shall not make haste.' 'In patience possess ye your souls.' On the other hand, the sacrifice of our Lord—His devotion, His enthusiasm, His care for the least, His gift of Himself for the lowest—makes it impossible for His followers to do nothing. 'Fight the good fight.' 'Be vigilant.' 'Man must be a fighter ever.' If there is one unhappy amid the ninety-nine who are happy, if there is one who is wretched, wilful, lazy, or drunken, amid the crowd of the willing and sober, the Christian must leave the ninety-nine and go after the one. The most undeserving has the greatest claim.

They who take Christ into themselves are bound to be here as those who serve. We may see that struggle and death work out good; we may mark the exaggerations of enthusiasts or partisans; but as long as we see one brother in need, the memory of our Lord's gift constrains us. He gave Himself, and we must give ourselves. The Christian's question is always, 'Master, what can I do?'

Systems which have done most to raise humanity have not been those which have stirred anger against society, or levelled accusations against a class with the cry of, 'Ours the rights, yours the faults.' Systems which have advanced the world have been those which have roused a man against himself, forced the confession, 'Mine the fault,' and raised the cry of Duty. They, as Mazzini has taught us, who fight only for their rights forget their duties to others, and become in their turn tyrants.

Successful reforms have always been in essence puritan—the work of men who, as individuals, have fought evil in themselves. Christianity aims to purify the individual. It says to him when he accuses others, 'Judge thyself.' It calls him to begin with self-reform—to take the beam out of his own eye if he would take the mote from his brother's eye. Its teaching is, 'Thou must be born again.' And, as Dean Stanley says, '"Thou art the man" is or ought to be—expressed or unexpressed—the conclusion of every practical sermon.'

Christ still leads His followers one by one, and he who feels His presence asks, not, 'What ought *they* to do?' but, 'What can I do?'

As citizen, as employer, as employed, as neighbour—

each who calls himself Christian must ask, 'What can I do for the unemployed?'

1. As a citizen I can vote for the general interest, and not for that of myself or my class. The privileges of a few make the hardship of the many. If the privileges by which some benefit were removed, there might be more work for others. I can vote for better education. If everyone had his intellect awakened and his tastes developed, there would not be so many incapable of responsibility, or so unfit for country life. I can vote for the provision of training for the unskilled and of discipline for the unwilling. It is want of strength or skill which prevents many from doing work. If another chance of acquiring such skill were offered, there might be more men fit to relieve those who are now overworked. If each voter in his vote bore others' burdens —fulfilling the law of Christ—some needs of the unemployed would be met.

2. As an employer I can see that every one I employ receives a wage adequate to support life. It is not sufficient to give the market rate or even what the union requires. The responsibility is the employer's. He is not justified if a woman receives 10s. or 12s. a week. He knows this wage is inadequate to support life in its sickness and age. It is not sufficient either for a member of a company to throw the responsibility on the shareholders; he is himself responsible, and must agitate for adequate wages as for an adequate dividend. If each employer thought of his servant as Christ thinks of him, the half employed would not now offer a sight so disgraceful to our humanity.

3. As employed I can see that I put in good work, keep regular hours and fill up my time. The example of irregularity and the practice of dawdling so as to spin out jobs, or of scamping so as to insure their renewal, encourage weaker natures in courses which lead to loss of work. Many of the unemployed owe their condition to the bad example of their first shops. If each Christian did his

work with all his might, as for God and not for man, there would be fewer wayward and unstable characters unable to do continuous work.

4. As a neighbour I can befriend a neighbour. Everybody knows one who is weak, wilful, or drunken; let him devote himself to that one with the persistency and the faithfulness and the sympathy of Christ; let him leave off dealing with masses and giving to beggars; let him hold on to the one, till by sacrifice of money, time, or holidays, he *convinces* him of his care. A limit would soon be put on his luxury which absorbs capital and embitters human relations. How could he who cared for his neighbour, and believed that money might help his need, spend that money on fancy foods or fancy furniture? Love is the only conqueror. The rich man who knows his poor neighbour, not by reports but as a friend, will not use in ostentation the wealth by which the neighbour could be strengthened. The poor man who knows his rich neighbour, not by subscription lists or gifts, but as a friend, will be conscious of a new force urging him to hope and effort. If every one who calls himself Christian would convince his neighbour not simply of his goodwill, but of a love which beareth all things, believeth all things, hopeth all things, endureth all things, many a man who is hopeless and therefore unemployed, would become a happy worker. Conviction of love is the first step in conversion.

Christians as citizens, as employers, as employed, as neighbours, must do all these things and more than these things. Christianity does not provide a code of social duty. It does not say what is the limit of luxury, and it does not fix the living wage. Christianity is Christ's spirit, and it is too large to be shut up in any law or set of rules. Christ's spirit is always progressing, guiding men into new truth. It attacks the individual, taking by storm this man to-day, that man to-morrow; its presence is first visible in the rise of public opinion, and afterwards it takes shape in law or rules of conduct. But the law and the rules are only for a time, they have to be repealed when the progressing spirit requires actions which are higher and more loving. Each Christian, as a follower of Christ, must obey His spirit, if the common action—the law—is to be helpful. Individual responsibility is the corner-stone of progress.

We as Christians believe that it is not just a leader, a great social reformer, a devoted man, who calls us to help the weak. We believe that the voice of God speaks through Christ. The Almighty has through the ages thundered out His wrath against the selfish and the careless. He has sought the successful in the hour of their pride and their security. He has asked the question, 'Where is thy brother?' Nations and individuals have dared to answer, 'Am I my brother's keeper?' and they, daring, have been cast out and overthrown. Their epitaph may always be read, 'He was not here as one who served.' The Almighty has declared His will amid thunder and lightning, by the decline and fall of nations, in the strife of war and in the despair of the fallen, but He has let His will reach us through Christ. By the pressure of that presence each man is drawn to love; by the voice which speaks to him as to an individual, he is summoned to serve his neighbour; by a call which is directed straight to himself and to no other, he is sent to do his work. God reaches the individual through His Son, and through the individual comes universal happiness.

We, men and women, individuals distinct in thought, feeling, and experience, stand amid the unemployed, 'the vast army of the homeless and unfed.' Our hearts are moved by the sight of such sorrow, and our anger is roused that such starvation should be in the midst of plenty. 'Why,' we ask, 'do these little ones suffer?' 'Why are these desolate and unfriended?' 'Why are there so many weak, vicious and bitter?' 'Surely they who by their selfishness have caused these things shall be punished.' Who are they? A voice which whispers to each of us, 'Thou art the man!' is the voice of God.

WOMEN'S WORK.

BY THE

REV. E. HOSKYNS,
RECTOR OF STEPNEY.

'*Son, behold thy mother.*'—ST. JOHN xix. 27.

APPROACH the subject with one or two preliminary questions.

What is our idea of woman?

Subdivide:

a. What is an employer's idea of woman?

b. What is a working man's idea of woman?

c. What is woman's idea of woman?

It is impossible for me to answer such questions; but when one reads such a Blue-book as that lately issued on women's work, the question is forced home again and again: What has an employer passing through his mind when he seems by his action to say, 'I must have this or that for men, but anything is good enough for women—any wages, any hours, any standard of comfort, any sanitation'?

Or, again, what is passing through the minds of our working men, even our trades unionists, when they fight for their own hand and grasp their eight-hours day or forty-eight hours a week, but let their young daughters slave for seventy-four to eighty hours, and their wives needle-drive until eleven and twelve at night?

And yet once more, what is woman's idea of woman, when she seems to hug the position into which she is placed, and take as her due the office of hewer of wood and drawer of water, or that of a scolded housekeeper, not a wife? How soon this acceptance of a low standard leads to all loss of modesty and true womanhood we know too well.

Generally speaking, I assert that man's view of woman is low, and that you will see the effect of such a view most clearly in the conditions under which man is willing that woman should work. True that we want laws; but above all we want 'gentlemen,' and that not confined to any class or rank, but managers, husbands, foremen, officials, whose conduct is considerate and gentle towards woman.

It is our duty as men—it ought to be our pride—to guard women against the crushing weight of manufactural stress. For us to seize the advantages, and to place woman as a buffer to bear the burdens and to receive into her bosom all the sharpest pangs of labour-pressure—this is beneath contempt.

Brothers, for a moment let us consider various reasons why, when we ask woman to work for us, we should be considerate.

1. What a debt of *gratitude* we owe to woman, and this quite apart from her position as mother!

Think of that wonderful profession for women—the nurses of our childhood, the daughters of our working men—so faithful, so patient, so noble in their self-denial!

Or, again, call to mind that army of teachers into whose hands is given the moulding of our children, and destined to become even still more the guardians of our boys in the lower standards of our boys' schools.

Or, again, have we no feelings of gratitude as we remember that noble profession of deaconness and sister, of nurses in hospital, in home, in parish, bringing to the sick and wearied of our cities not only skill, but oftentimes a love which these poor men have, as they say, never tasted before? Or, when we look out on the great world of commerce, in counting-house, in work-room, in factory, what a place must we give to women! See them streaming from every street converging on the City, hear the clang of the wooden shoon in the North, all adding to the national wealth, all serving us men in ways which touch us at every point, and then say whether gratitude is not deserved.

2. But gratitude by itself will not survive the daily rush and turmoil of the factory. Your young employer, your anxious foreman, only sees hands, hands, hands—not a face, not a body, not a life, which can grow weary; but hands which are nimble and do the work quickly, and grasp less on the Saturday than the hand of a man.

It is not reason to expect that gratitude is enough here, and so we appeal to men for *sympathy*. We ask men, and especially employers of labour, working men, and the purchasing public, to remember the simple fact that woman is physically weaker than man for that kind of labour too often put upon her, and that the results of overstrain are far more terrible in the case of woman. Hence, from an economic view, the folly of bad conditions, long hours, low wages, all tending to lower the producing power. But surely sympathy becomes the more necessary when we recollect that woman, in addition to all her natural weakness and greater proneness to pain, is called also to be the mother of mankind! Here is a national question, then, of prime importance, affecting the national life in a marked degree. For this reason do we demand that sympathy for woman should penetrate even into the secret chambers of Boards and of Cabinets.

Who, then, will not sympathize with the young girl in that drapery establishment? You look in early in the morning; there she is, standing and arranging the goods, after lifting down heavy weights quite beyond her strength. In the afternoon, *still* in the same position; at 6, still standing; at 8.30, still standing; on Saturday at 9, 10, 11, still standing; and then look at her anæmic face, and ask yourself, What is the real reason that allows such conditions to be in force? And so I might take you, had I the time, through factory and restaurant, through laundry and white-lead works, and into the homes of our home-workers, at 11, 12, and 1 at night. I might show you the brightest instances of factories and workrooms, where all is well; but I might read to you pages of evidence revealing the circumstances under which our women work, where nothing is done except by compulsion; where every advantage is taken of the weakness of women; where ordinary decency is impossible; where all the instincts of womanhood are crushed, and woman is treated as a cheap machine.

But it is not only, or especially, the weakness of woman which appeals, or should appeal, to the true manliness of man. It is the great fact that woman is called to the high office of wife and mother (the *real* mother, who not only bears but *rears* the child), and in this capacity, Ruskin says, is the great producer of wealth.

'It is not good for man to be alone: I will make him an helpmeet for him.' And the man is to say, 'This is now bone of my bone and flesh of my flesh. Therefore shall a man leave his father and mother, and shall cleave unto his wife, and they shall be one flesh.' Back to this primitive law of marriage, after the intervening period of polygamy, Christ brings us, and Christianity, if it is true to the Master, will go up to the fountain-head of social life, casting salt in there, checking all license, and placing woman in her right and lawful position—the partner and companion of man. And because of this high vocation of woman, we men are called upon to show 'gentle consideration' towards the wife.

But surely our duty lies beyond our own home. You cannot as a Churchman or a citizen look out upon the homes of our people, you cannot as employers arrange your business, with eyes closed to this great factor in the matter.

What shall we say, then, as to methods and systems which make it all but impossible to produce happy wives or healthy mothers? To a great extent a happy home depends upon health; but to how many of our young wives health has gone ere marriage comes! In two or three years they are the jaded, wearied mothers, with hardly spirit to clean the home or tend the children. No wonder that the children are poor little weaklings, dwarfed in body and warped in mind, a danger to the State, a dishonour to God!

And, if rightly understood, how will this question affect the attitude of working men? More and more they will find that it is far better to have a clean home and mothered children, than a home dirty and neglected, children untidy and disobedient, because the wife works at the factory. In many places both masters and men agree that married women shall not continue in the factory; but in too many places still the wives of men who are earning large wages continue to work, and so neglect their homes, forsake their children, and too often create a loafing and lazy manhood, only too pleased to be idle and to live on the hard-earned wages of the wife.

I say this is to sap the very root of national health and wealth, and is to follow the base example of some of our high-born mothers at the other end of the social scale, who cannot brook the delay necessary for the feeding and care of their child, so strong is the claim that society has upon them. The punishment to all mothers, of all classes, is sure and bitter. Too often they never taste of the joy of a true mother's love; they never receive a child's devotion; children never rise up to call them blessed, for their mothers spurned them from their bosoms, and forgat their work.

To preserve, then, the high place accorded to woman will be the care of all men, especially those in authority. The nation will do everything to preserve the home, and the Church will arouse the consciences of all her sons to bear in mind the sanctity, the grace of marriage.

And yet once more, as we ask why we should respect and consider woman, it is enough for us who are gathered together to-day under the ægis of a union which boasts the name of Christian, to call to remembrance the great fact that He whom we love and worship as God was *born of woman*—Mary, the *Mother* of Jesus!

Before this mystery we men bow our heads. We were not called to share in that marvellous childhood.

We only can stand at a distance and catch the words of Gabriel as he announces to the Virgin Mary the great doctrine which the Church exists to proclaim, ' Hail, thou that art highly favoured, the Lord is with thee: blessed art thou amongst women. The Holy Ghost shall come upon thee, and the power of the Highest shall overshadow thee; therefore that holy thing which shall be born of thee shall be called the Son of God.'

Or we shall listen to that great vesper hymn as it welled forth from the heart of the Blessed Virgin, the *Magnificat*, proclaiming as it does not only the rights of man, but the emancipation of woman.

Or, and this would be well, we will catch of the spirit of Joseph, who in the midst of doubt and disappointment saw that it was his highest office as a man and a husband to guard woman and wife from the slanders and the dangers of the world.

How natural, then, that we should to-day bring that honour and reverence which is due to the Mother of our Lord! But we cannot stay there. Thoughts of her will lead us to view all women differently, and we shall take to ourselves the solemn charge with a new meaning: 'Son, behold thy mother.'

Do you say, 'Ah, this is fanciful and idealistic'? We, too, like to contemplate the Madonna and Holy Child, but go and see that stream of jam-factory girls; listen to the language of those match girls; do you see those rag-sorters? Yes, I do see them; and just because I have known many of them, and just because it has been my lot to be acquainted with women who have risen above all the miserable conditions under which they have worked, I am able to say that there is no reason for such miserable pessimism, and that the sights and sounds which too often haunt us are the direct outcome of the inconsiderateness of man.

And if you say, Well, then, be practical, and put laws upon the Statute Book; I reply, By all means put them there, but for God's sake *keep* them. Send inspectors and inspectresses. Yes, *do*, especially the latter; but what then?

You have got some better conditions, and you have got, and that is what we want, *knowledge;* but, then, we require the voice of the Church to arouse the consciences of our men, and to awaken in their breasts true Christian chivalry.

It is here that it appears to me we need a loud and clear call. It is man's duty to be to the front in defending woman.

Trades union men must fight the battle, not for themselves, but for the women. Better for them to be slower in winning their own ends than to leave woman in the rear of the labour movement to be harassed and maltreated.

Is there no truth in the words of a mother in my parish, as I entered a room and found her at tea with her son at 6.30? 'There's my daughter goes out an hour before him, and comes back an hour and a half after him, and gets 10s. less; but the men are so selfish.'

It is not laws only but true religion which is needed here, something which will inspire all men with true nobility of character, and make them true knights of labour. Oh, we want in our great Christian society to-day another great baptismal question, 'Will you train up this boy to respect woman?' to be pressed home in confirmation, 'Will you promise in every way possible to respect woman?'

I have held this morning that the question of the conditions under which women work resolves itself into the question, What does man think of woman? and I affirmed that man's idea of woman is low. I dare not close my subject without clenching the argument, and proving it to the hilt.

What shall we say of man's cruelty and meanness as he creates that ghastly profession of the harlot? Man, too selfish to marry, enjoying the independence, the luxury of his club, yet takes advantage of woman's position, and, her natural guardian, wilfully betrays her.

Here is England's curse, to which drunkenness is nothing.

But the question which I want to ask is this, What is the connection between low wages and immorality? Is work given out at an abominable wage because it is known that it can be done, for other wages are earned?

Undoubtedly there are cases where an employer ought to say, 'Seeing the condition of my employés, I must either raise the wages and take from them their awful temptation, or I must close the works.'

Or, again, do women ever say, 'I can undersell another woman, and carry out that order at a starvation price, because those wages are not all I earn?'

Then, I say, all honour to any society, any union, any legislation, which says, 'This shall not be.'

Do I lift the veil here in a dark spot? I must go lower still, where woman is still more at the mercy of man, and where we can still better gauge his real opinion of woman.

Come away from that abominable scene in central London every night in the year (a scene which by itself proves my point); leave the sham gaiety of it all, follow me. Come up these dirty stairs in that back street, knock at the door, and behold that girl lying there, soon to be the victim of consumption. She still struggles out, but now with thick veil. 'She must live,' she cries, or as one said to me last week, 'I don't mean mother to go into the workhouse.'

But ask her her history. It is the history of many members of one of the largest branches of women's professions.

'I was a servant, and I fell through my master,' or his son. I am speaking within bounds and within knowledge when I say that domestic servants suffer most at the hands of men, cruel and unscrupulous in their conduct.

Why cannot we men, whose talk is now so constantly upon social questions, begin where it is possible to-day?

Are we really in earnest, or are we merely pandering to a mere cry which is for the moment popular? To-day, to-day, we might stay the tears of many a wounded soul, and check the early death of many a wounded body, if only we would accept the Master's charge, to defend and honour woman.

Only one word would I add, a word of encouragement. It is not all dark. It is the very excellence of many workshops and factories which enables us to see what is possible and whets our appetite for more of such.

Again and again do I receive evidence of the genuine interest taken in girls in the City. Where do we clergy in the East End and in our Northern towns look for Sunday-school teachers, and even visitors? It is to those who seem to have triumphed over all difficulties, and have gained through their very trials a strong independence of character. In tone, in strength of will, they call forth our admiration, and as wives and mothers become our one hope in the midst often of dreary and depressing surroundings.

And as woman is more and more demanding from us men the respect due to her, as she is refusing to be treated as the mere sport and toy of men, let us men rise also to our office, and together with them labour for a brighter and purer citizenship.

SPECULATION.

BY THE

REV. WILFRID RICHMOND,

AUTHOR OF 'ECONOMIC MORALS.'

'If any would not work, neither should he eat.'—2 THESS. iii. 10.

WHY not? If he could get anyone to feed him for nothing, why should he not accept the gift and be thankful? St. Paul was appealing to a principle recognised among the Jews, a principle to which he had already appealed before. In a country which bred parasites, those who were content to feed on the bounty of the great or of their friends, the Christian Church had its parasites, too—parasites on the organized charity of her social life. St. Paul had already invoked the Jewish maxim, familiar to himself and other Jews, that if any would not work neither should he eat.

The maxim is no less recognised among ourselves. We, too, attempt so to organize our charity—though there is not quite so much of it to organize—we, too, try to avoid any violation of the principle, that if any man will not work neither shall he eat. But it is worth while asking—why not? Why do we think it wrong that a man should eat without working? Why is 'parasite' a term of reproach? It is not merely that work is a good thing in itself. If a man were offered the choice between life in a lazy, lotus-eating land, where no labour was needed to gain the means of living, and a life which would employ the energies of body and of mind, and would give him the same provision for his needs as the reward, we should despise the man who chose the lazy rather than the active life. But this is not the reproach against the parasite. We blame the parasite, not because he is lazy, but because he is a fraud. He eats without working ; he gets without giving.

We acknowledge, then, in one part of our social life, this principle. If you get without giving, you are a fraud on society. Without giving—not merely without working. If a man digs a hole in the earth and fills it up again, that, in fact, is not work. We do not call work 'work' unless it is work for which someone is the better. The principle on which we blame the parasite is this—you have no right to take from society, or from any individual, the means of life, unless it be in return for something by which they are the gainers. For the moment, and for this particular purpose, it does not matter whether we look at the question from the social point of view, and say a man has no right to his share of the produce of the common labour unless he has done his part in the common labour ; or whether we say a man has no right to take from the individual man what belongs to him unless he has given him something in exchange. Either way of putting it leaves us the same question to be addressed to those who live by any given occupation. You eat : what is your work ? You get : what do you give ? Is the society in or on which you live any the better for you ? Does the individual who contributes to your income get anything in return ? Or are *you* a parasite ?

And the question is to be asked, obviously, not of those only who derive their whole income from any particular source that may be in question, but as to any part of a man's income it may be asked, Is it the reward of work ? What has been given for it ? Let us take one instance in the matter that is before us to-day—speculation.

We clergy are said to be not averse to speculation. Certainly they send us circulars enough as to speculative investments. Take the case, then, of a country parson. His professional income, from tithe or glebe land, has diminished. He finds himself face to face with hopeless difficulties. Very likely he married imprudently. Very likely he started in life with college debts. Equip him with all the vices necessary to heighten the colour of the picture. It is all his fault—that makes him the more disposed to run a risk. Anyhow, one morning, he leaves his parish and his schools, he looks into his affairs, he sees ruin not far off. And that same morning there has arrived a very tempting circular. He must have some money somehow; he yields to the temptation; he sells out from some safe investment; he runs the risk. What is the result? He loses, you say, and he deserves to be called a fool for his pains. I don't care whether he loses or not. I want to know, not whether he is a fool, but whether he is a knave. Suppose he does not lose, but gains. What is the result then? What has he done? *He* knows, or he ought to know. He has to answer the question: Where did the money come from?—the money which he must have—somehow, and which he has got—somehow. The labourers in his parish live on their wages, as best they may, and week by week leave something done—something by which the world, or their small corner of it, is the better for them. The farmer lives off his farm as best he may; and he, too, is living by the work of his own hand and brain, and has something to show for it, something for which he is paid. The village shopkeeper lives by bringing the produce of the labour of others within reach of his neighbours. The doctor lives by ministering to the wants of others. Hitherto the parson himself has done the same. We will suppose the labourer to have been worthy of his hire. The squire—well, there are several ways of it with the squire. He may be well-to-do—though he is not always that—but he may be well-to-do, and yet do a day's work among his neighbours, which is cheap enough at the price of the income he lives on. Or he may do nothing in return for his living, and in that case the parson knows what he ought to have told him, if it were not rather difficult to tell—a home-truth or so out of the Bible, such as this, 'If any man would not work, neither should he eat.'

There may be a banker or a merchant from a neighbouring town, who, if the parson had gone to him in his difficulties, would have given him—most excellent advice, not to risk his money in investments which he knew nothing about. It may be that he is plainly living on the fruit of labour by which the world has gained, and in that case he, too, adds to the rebuke; or it may be that *he* made his money—somehow, and in that case the parson will not feel much the better for being morally in the same boat with him.

But the life in the midst of which he lives teaches him that, in yielding to the desire to get money without regard to where it comes from, he has yielded to the desire to get money without giving anything in return, and that the question, where the money has come from, can only be answered by saying that it has come out of someone else's pocket. To get money somehow, anyhow — that is the passion to which speculation appeals. There may be cases with speculation, as with gambling, where the money is not the attraction, but the excitement—the chance—like the pleasure of a strong swimmer bathing in a stormy sea. Men delight in exercising their faculties, in being equal to emergencies, in calculating chances, in providing for and meeting contingencies. There may be cases where it is no conscious principle to gain by the loss of others. The gambler and the speculator alike, taking them in the mass, are full of the passion for money, and do gain, and know that they gain, by the loss of others, and by the loss of others only. But the passion which is really characteristic of the gambler and speculator alike is the love of chance—the delight in a world where law is not. And the professional gambler and speculator lives on a milder form of this passion which prevails among the mass of mankind—the desire to make money apart from the one law which regulates gain—the law of justice; the law of *quid pro quo;* the desire to make money somehow, anyhow.

It is not necessary to enter on any question as to whether interest on invested money is *ever* rightly earned. We may leave that question, at least for the sake of argument, on the footing that you have the same right to a continued and progressively increasing reward for past labour, when you hand on the use of the fruit of past labour to another instead of keeping it yourself. And if investment is allowed, a market for investments is allowed, and the merchant of stocks earns his living as justly as the merchant of cloth or of bread. But speculation in stocks and trade in stocks are two different things. They shade off into one another as night into day; but we know night from day all the same, and trade from speculation. And the simple question to be asked about speculation is this: You are reaping a reward; have you rendered a service?

No doubt it is possible to put cases which it would be very difficult to bring under the rule—cases where the speculator, following the precedent of Joseph in Egypt, foresees and provides for a future contingency, benefits society, and has earned by his foresight the further benefit which he gains for himself. To any such difficulties I would answer, first, that religion and morality deal with motives, and that the question is: Are you yielding to the passion for making money by calculating the chances of time? Are you yielding to the passion for making money, somehow, anyhow, independently of any question whether you have earned it or not? And I would answer, secondly, For the present I will be quite content to leave the doubtful cases. Deal with the cases where there is *no* doubt. Set to yourself this question, How do I make the income I live on? At the expense of those with whom I deal, or as the reward for some service I have rendered them? Every bargain ought to be to the benefit of both parties to the bargain. We need not be too nice about who gets the best of the bargain —the larger share of the benefit. The man with whom you deal wouldn't deal at all unless he thought he got *some* benefit. You keep the books of your business. There are duplicate books elsewhere. All that you receive is entered there the same. Your receipts, your income has been just what you have entered yourself. But in the duplicate books I speak of the opposite page will be a blank wherever you have received and given no real return. And the man with whom this has been so has been a parasite and hypocrite as well, deceiving the world, deceiving himself, but not deceiving the judgment of God.

Or set to yourself this deeper question. Here is the passion, the poison, of speculation exposed. It means defrauding your neighbours. It means gaining without giving. It means, in however exalted a fashion, living by your wits. The passion itself, the desire to make money, somehow, anyhow, is a passion widely spread. Is it in you? Is it a poison in your life? Is it a curse on your business? We have seen the evil of it writ large of late. We have seen it as the inspiration of villainy. We have seen it as some relentless monster of vice, feeding on the virtues of simplicity and thrift and trust, spreading piteous ruin among the poor, the helpless, and the weak. What was the soul of this vast and bloated fraud? You have joined the chorus of abhorrence and condemnation. What have you condemned? *Do* you abhor, shrink from, in yourself, in your own life, in your own business, the motive that was at work? In the development of trade and industry in the last hundred years great fortunes have been made before our eyes, as it seemed, by chance, by luck, without labour, almost without time. Our fancy catches at the instances of this. Our imagination is impressed. We dream of fortunes, and then this desire, this passion, lays hold of us, for money unearned, for money that is somehow to come to us. The man who walked through his vineyard and saw across the fence his neighbour's vineyard, and desired to have it, was a frankly covetous man. It is possible to be equally covetous without being equally frank. If you desire wealth, and mean to earn it, you desire the gift of God, according to the laws by which He gives it, the laws of labour and of justice. But if you desire wealth that shall come to you without the need of labour or the award of justice, you are only turning your back on the fence, you are coveting just the same. And if you gain what you desire, there are only two ways in which you can gain it—you can gain it from God as the reward of labour, justly paid by your neighbour, who shares with you the multiplied fruit of the labours which God so rewards; or you may gain it by what are, in fact, nothing else than the old and tried methods of the covetous man, falsehood and robbery and wrong. Is this disguised covetousness at work in you? Are you tainted by the poison? Are you content to *earn* money, and in your business to walk in the ways of God, who multiplies His gifts to men? Or are you not content with the multiplied gifts of God? Are you seeking to escape into a world where there is no God and no law, but only chance? The choice does not lie between God and chance, but between God and the devil. And the first and last word to be said about speculation is this: In its first beginnings, in the wild dream of fortune, in the instinctive longing for enrichment, no less truly than in the intricate and unscrupulous schemes of a deliberately fraudulent undertaking, it is nothing else but the desire to gain what you have not earned. It means, if you attempt it, that you throw off the rule of God. It means, if you succeed, that you rob your fellow-men.

'What am I to do? You are preaching against a system, and you are preaching to individuals entangled in the system, unable to shake themselves free and to take a line of their own.' I know that it is so. I know of men of business who have come to the clergy and said, 'I cannot become a communicant; the methods on which my business is conducted forbid it.' I know of young men starting in life, boys who have been prepared for Confirmation, who have come to the clergy and said, 'All that you have told me I see to be good, but when my chief gives me instructions which go against the laws of justice and truth, what am I to do?'

Exoriare aliquis! Oh for a voice to rouse the conscience, not of an individual here and there, but of a community—to rouse a collective conscience, quite content with a generally diffused dishonesty, under cover of an occasional outburst of hysterical indignation against offenders sufficiently flagrant to be found out. What are you to do? Thank God at least that He has led you to ask the question, if you ask it in earnest. Who knows how near we may be to the time when the community shall turn upon the system, and say this is not to be endured, and shall refuse to enforce the payment of a debt where it cannot equitably be said that any consideration has been received? If it be true to say that under our present commercial system the individual man cannot hope in many kinds of business to live up to the plain standard of honesty and truth, one need not be much of a socialist to say that here is a case for the State to intervene in any way that may be possible. One need not be much of a prophet to say that when the conscience of the community is roused to appreciate the facts, the remedy will not be far away.

But meanwhile what are you to do?

Above the shifting tides of City life, above the interlacing hurrying crowds, and all the turmoil and confusion of the devices and desires of men, on the top of the great dome of St. Paul's, there is set up the Cross of Christ. Look up to it; think what it means of loyalty to righteousness and truth, loyalty at any sacrifice and at any cost, and tell me— Could any minister of Christ, speaking of what we commonly call speculation, have claimed from you a less, a lower, loyalty to the eternal laws of justice and right than I have claimed to-day? My first business has been to draw the clear line between right and wrong.

And having done that, having said my say thus far, I dare not say less to the individual man than this. Here is the truth. Argue it out with yourself. Acknowledge the truth; set your face towards the light, and move towards it as you may. What your first step should be, and when you should take it, I cannot tell you. Your own conscience can. Oh for a voice, I said, to rouse the conscience of the community! Oh for a man, rather, to see and do the right whatever may come of it! It may be there is little you can do at once. Do something, at least. If for a time you have to bow yourself in the house of Mammon, I dare not tell you, looking up to the Cross, that He will deny you before His Father which is in heaven. But are you content to have it so?

We are close on Passion-tide. It is the time of all others to learn courage. I do not plead with you to have the courage to be true to yourself and to the standard of what you know to be right. I do not plead with you to recover your own self-respect, or to rise to an abstract standard of righteousness and justice. It is not for this that I ask you to have the courage to live by what you know to be the truth.

I plead with you for pity on the poor; the wronged, who often do not know that they are wronged, who from the midst of ruined lives, crying out against the hardness of fate, curse God and die. I plead with you for those who are deluded—the fools, whom those who are wiser pillage and despise; less fools, perhaps, than they who all along have said in their hearts, There is chance; there is no God. I plead with you for those who may perhaps have been sinners like yourselves, in that they, too, wished to make money anyhow they might, but sinners not against the same degree of light as you—rather led astray by you, who know what business is.

I ask you simply to take the stories of the victims of the Liberator frauds, as we have all read them, and to say to yourself, This and the like of this is going on every day, not always on the same scale, not always with the same degree of flagrant fraud, but in the essence of it this very thing over and over again. On the one hand the ignorant speculator, often not even knowing that he is a speculator at all, and on the other hand the skilled speculator, knowing very well that he renders neither to man nor God any service for which he should be paid; and the pockets of the ignorant speculator are emptied that the pockets of his wiser brother may be filled.

I plead with you to say for yourself that you, for your part, will have neither part nor lot in such a system; that inch by inch, as you see your opportunity, you will fight the battle against it—fight for pity against cruel wrong; fight for truth against the falsehood which is murdering generation after generation of the souls of the young; fight for justice, to make the honesty of English commerce as much a proverb as the righteousness of English rule.

'SOLDIERS AND SAILORS.'

BY THE

REV. R. R. DOLLING,
HEAD OF WINCHESTER COLLEGE MISSION, PORTSMOUTH.

'One soweth, and another reapeth.'
—JOHN iv. 38.

GENTLEMEN, I must begin by making the awful and solemn declaration that after eighteen centuries of Christianity the object of the 'Prince of Peace' has not been attained. War still exists, and therefore it is necessary to speak of soldiers and sailors.

But the Divine Carpenter will have His revenge, and His revenge will be complete when by means of labour, which He emancipated and glorified, war shall cease throughout the whole world. In a large measure, labour is already organized in England, and the working man is learning day by day his own value, but this is at best but a partial step towards peace, and it needs that the English example should be followed upon the Continent, and the movement become cosmopolitan. When once the foreign workman has realized his own powers—powers which, surely, we can teach him can be asserted without anarchy and the disruption of society—when shameful wages and shameful hours and the abominable sweating system, depriving men of the fruits of their labours, shall have ceased universally, as they have begun to cease in England, then the patient pleadings of the Carpenter of Nazareth will be realized, and man—the temporal redeemer of the earth by the sweat of his brow—shall refuse to be manipulated as the enemy of his brethren, either in the sweating dens of financiers, or on the battle-fields, or in the armies, maintained at present at an impossible cost by politicians or by monarchs, for their own selfish purpose.

The Carpenter will have His revenge, and therefore it is not Utopian to suppose that a day will come when war shall cease.

But while it is well to have these higher ideals before us, it is certainly foolish not to look things in the face and realize what they are at the present moment. And, above all, it is our duty, as their employers, to recognise the crushing evils which to-day exist among our soldiers and sailors.

And standing in the very centre of the world's market, it is well for us to confess that these men have laboured, and that you, the merchants of England, have entered into their labours.

There is not a single vessel in your port of London, there is not a single article by the buying and selling of which you amass your fortunes, there is not a single pound the turning over of which adds to your riches, that you do not in the truest sense owe to their bravery and self-denial, and therefore, surely, it ought to be an undisputed fact that it is incumbent upon you to render the condition of their toil and life as harmless as possible.

Gentlemen, you live in your own homes surrounded by saintly women, the atmosphere of whose lives is to you a continual reminder of what you ought to be.

The pure influence of the Christian home (Christ's own method of creating men to follow the example of His own life), the home, the woman's influence, the little child's pleading ways, the very sight of your boys and girls growing up before you—these, the most potent helps for true self-government, the sailor and the soldier voluntarily surrender for your sake.

Is it too much, then, to say that their lives are passed in an unnatural state, in which it is almost impossible for them to lead a pure, noble, and godly life; though I am proud to say that, from my own experience, I know how many achieve splendid characters; but surely it is rather in spite of the disadvantages they suffer than in response to their daily environment.

But even looking at this matter from a selfish point of view, something should be done for the welfare of those who protect the country, else it will be found more increasingly difficult to recruit the ranks of the services.

If a number of great City merchants should supply money to build ironclads to fill the Thames, unless they considered the personnel of the navy, their ironclads would be in vain.

At the present moment, I believe, the Admiralty require nearly 10,000 men to man the ships they already have, and if that be true of the navy, it is also true of the sister service. How many army corps do you suppose at this present moment you could put in the field?

The continued drain of soldiers to their linked battalions in India and elsewhere leaves the strength of regiments at home little better than weedy boys, just recruited.

Gentlemen, what is the reason of this?

Is the spirit of adventure passing away from England? Surely not!

There is hardly an English lad who attains manhood, who has not at one time or another in his life dreamed of becoming either a soldier or a sailor.

Is the patriotic love of our country passing away? God forbid that any Englishman should think that. England, freer, nobler, more truly just, than she has ever been before, demands, and I believe receives, the love and loyalty of all her sons.

Why, then, does recruiting fail in both branches of the service?

The reasons are not difficult to find, though, owing to the mysterious system which prevails at the War Office and the Admiralty, great masses of the English people are kept in the dark on these vital questions : many do not even know that this deficiency exists.

The time has gone by when it is possible to recruit from the riffraff, when the soldier may be a mere machine.

Intelligence and acuteness are necessary for the fulfilment of many of the soldier's—and certainly of all the sailor's—duties; hence it is necessary to recruit from a better class, and to-day the service-man demands, and has a right to receive, a living wage.

This difficulty, to a certain extent, does not exist in the navy, for lads are caught young, before they know their true value; but the difficulty of recruiting stokers, who are enlisted at the age of eighteen, surely teaches us that a like difficulty would arise in recruiting bluejackets at the same age.

If your warships are to be increased, you must multiply your training-ships round the coast, and these training-ships, on which in a large measure depends the whole future of your navy, should be removed from centres of pollution and danger like Portsmouth, Devonport, etc, and placed in spots round the coast where the lads could live a far more natural life, with much more recreation in the fields—a life, in fact, purer and more wholesome in all ways than is at present possible.

Some of you may have sons on the *Britannia;* if so, you will doubtless be able to supply yourselves a true comment on this part of my story. Then the captains, lieutenants, and chaplains of these ships should be men of age and temperament, and special experience in understanding the aspirations and the dangers of youth ; not pitched into the berth because it happens to be their turn for such promotion, but selected, and then remaining in such special training service, so that the whole surrounding of the boy's life may be a sympathetic atmosphere, specially directed towards the minimizing of those dangers which of necessity must exist in his present homeless life.

But leaving this question of training, let us consider the question of wages.

A man is drawn into the ranks of the army on practically false—I say shamefully false—pretence. Nominally he receives a shilling a day and rations.

What are the facts? Threepence out of every shilling is stopped to supply extra food necessary for his bodily health, whether he will or no.

A halfpenny is compulsorily stopped for washing; thus his shilling becomes eightpence-halfpenny; but these deductions do not stop here: barrack damages, library, hair-cutting, and oftentimes other compulsory subscriptions, make a still further reduction, so that at the end of the week the shilling is seldom more than sevenpence.

Until he gets his shilling per day, and his accounts are simplified, so that he can easily understand the deductions made, you need never expect to enlist efficient and intelligent men. Again, he is supplied with a nominally free kit, but the uniform part, if it does not fit him, which is usually the case, is altered at his expense.

This kit is by Government renewed from time to time, but his under-kit, consisting of three pairs of socks, two shirts, two towels, one little bit of soap, and other things necessary for what is called cleaning, he has to maintain for seven long years.

He has to show his kit monthly, and if he is lacking in any of these articles, or they are not in good repair, he has to pay for new ones, and he is punished as well. From such causes I have often known a soldier driven into a state of practical sullen rebellion, out of heart with his profession, out of heart with his officers, a man most dangerous to himself and especially dangerous to the society in which he lives. This kit question must be settled upon an honourable basis.

Again, the present short service system is a great hindrance to recruiting.

The lodging-houses of England are full of those soldiers in the reserve living on their sixpence a day; seven years, the best of their lives, have been taken, rendering them unfit (according to the testimony of employers of labour) for ordinary work.

The deferred pay—amounting to £21—is just enough to allow them to revel in a month or two of debauch, not enough to enable them to set up in any useful business. Of course there are very many exceptions to this description, but there are a large number of these men loafing round public-houses, a continuous warning to mothers and fathers to prevent their boys from becoming soldiers or sailors.

The pay in the navy is a little in advance of that in the army, but there a man has to buy and keep up all his whole kit.

Very often a new captain demands a new kind of rig, and so men are being constantly put to a practically unnecessary expense.

Even a chief petty officer, who after qualifying in gunnery and torpedoes and diving, becomes gunnery instructor, and then captain of a turret, only receives five shillings and a penny per day. This is a man of such true intelligence and attainment that in civil life he would be receiving a very large salary. It is fair, of course, to add that he has a pension in view, but so few men attain all these qualifications that they hardly affect the question.

But it is not merely a question of pay; it is surely a question of risk as well.

These men carry their lives in their hands for your sakes. It is a noble thing truly to die for one's country, but if you leave wife and children behind to beggary, and worse, surely the country does not fulfil her part of the bargain.

I need not refer to the shameful management of the Patriotic and *Victoria* Funds; but shameful as is the provision made for widows and orphans in the *Victoria* case, happy, you may say, is the woman whose husband happens to die in a crowd; if he had fallen overboard on some stormy night, or been killed pursuing a slaver on the African coast, his wife and children would have got nothing at all.

It is this awful uncertainty about the future of those he loves best that is a continual menace to the peace of mind of the soldier and sailor. One little incident will illustrate the heartlessness and cruelty of the Admiralty.

A man's kit is his own; if he dies on board ship it is auctioned on board amongst his comrades, who always pay a great deal more than its value, and send the money home as a loving present to his friends.

But because the *Victoria* went down, the men who were lost in her had no compensation allowed to their relatives. The men who lived got something inadequately small. It is this red-tape of the Whitehall officials that strangles the loyalty of the bluejacket.

But there are other difficulties which I am bound, though unwillingly, to mention. Practically, marriage is forbidden to the soldier; at least, for the first five years of his service, and then only a few are allowed on the strength of the regiment. God's Apostle says, 'It is better to marry than to burn.' Many of these men marry. Out of their pay of sevenpence per day, what can they give their wives? It means that the wife has no recognised claim for support on her husband at all. Either she tries to follow the regiment at her own expense, with the chance of being sent back by the Government, or drags on a miserable existence — married, yet practically unmarried. It is almost impossible to imagine the lives of these women, as they are spent in Portsmouth and other military centres.

The sailor, on the other hand, is allowed to marry, and a certain portion of his pay he can allot to his wife; but when I tell you that in the case of an ordinary seaman this amounts to £1 per month, and as his rating increases a little more is added, I need hardly do more than ask you to imagine what a wife with little children can do under circumstances like these.

If wrong comes of it, and Jack (who for our sakes has practically surrendered wife and children) receives a wound to his honour which is worse than death, a very stab in his heart, gentlemen, on whom lies the blame?

But there is another side of the question worse than marriage.

Think of those strong, vigorous, well-groomed, fairly-fed men, with all to make their body strong, their passions powerful, think of them living separated altogether from womankind, with the common talk of the barrack-room, or of the lower deck, ever sounding in their ears, centred in such sinks of iniquity as Portsmouth, Plymouth, Chatham, Aldershot, and other garrison towns, where the streets are beyond measure disgraceful.

In Portsmouth, for instance, which I know well, there are to be found on the Hard, at the very Dockyard gates, no less than fourteen buildings constructed and carried on for the sale of intoxicating drinks, twelve being fully-licensed houses, out of a total of twenty-six.

The post-office, where sailors have very frequently to go, stands between a group of seven, five being next door to each other on the one side, and two on the other. Out of the Hard opens Queen Street, the practical thoroughfare of Portsea, with a very large number of public-houses in it, and several alleys and courts—you can hardly call them streets—which are practically full of brothels.

Is it any wonder, then—to quote the words of his worship the Mayor of Portsmouth—'that even in this garrison there were nearly half the men in hospital, owing to the repeal of the C.D. Acts'?

Is it any wonder that the Admiralty and War Office have communicated with Lord Clanwilliam and the general commanding at Portsmouth and other garrison centres, telling them to take steps with the civil authorities to ameliorate these evils?

Is it any wonder that we, who know that in an awful sense

the sins of the fathers are visited upon the children from generation to generation, demand that some steps shall be taken? I do not say to re-enact the C.D. Acts—that is a matter of consideration—but to change the intolerable temptation that besets these lads, who for your sakes endure temptations to which the dangers of the battle-field are as nothing.

If you say that you supply them with a State-made and State-paid-for religion, I do not think you dare salve your conscience with such an excuse.

To create the priest into the officer, the free worship of Almighty God into a compulsory Queen's parade, is that the method to convert any soul to Christ, or build him up in the service of One whose worship is 'perfect freedom'? If you want to know about this, ask first for statistics of communions made by soldiers and sailors, or of their attendance made at voluntary services in the evening.

I am told it is far too common that at the evening voluntary service in garrison towns the soldier is conspicuous by his absence.

Gentlemen, I bless God that there are many noble, true-hearted Christian people working for the soldier and the sailor.

The names of Miss Robinson and Miss Weston will be familiar to you all, and many besides them—but I confess it with shame, as a priest of the Church of England, that, as a rule, these efforts have not been made by those in our own communion.

The Wesleyans, Undenominationals, Roman Catholics, put us to shame; but while confessing our shame, let us be encouraged to think that at last a movement has been made at Aldershot, at Gosport, at Pirbright, and in Woolwich, and perhaps in other towns I do not know—the Church of England Institute is in working order, not in a spirit of competition with those who have been in the field before, and for whose untiring labours we thank Almighty God, but striving to make up a little of the deficiency which to our shame exists. If you have money, I pray you give it to these institutions; but at any rate never let one single day pass without praying Almighty God that He may govern and direct the bodies and souls of soldiers and sailors in the way of everlasting life.

BETTING AND GAMBLING.

BY THE

REV. J. S. BARRASS,
RECTOR OF ST. MICHAEL, BASSISHAW.

GENTLEMEN, in the absence of the Rev. J. W. Horsley through illness, I have been called upon at short notice to address you on 'betting and gambling.' I shall take the subject from its popular side of 'wagering' on sporting events. Before doing so, I cannot pass by without comment the serious gambling which takes place 'on' and 'off' the Stock Exchange.

No one can deny that side by side with the genuine business of the Stock Exchange there is constantly going on a form of gambling. That that gambling is deplored by the best men on the Stock Exchange is conceded; but the fact remains, and a very damaging fact it is to those who seek to wage war against gambling, to have hurled at their heads that much of the commercial business of the country is carried on in the form of gambling. Surely this is degrading in the commercial world? And if this is so of the Stock Exchange, what is to be said of the business of the 'bucket-shop'? Surely no one will deny that gambling of a base and degrading character is carried on there. To denounce the system as a swindle is to speak of it in the accents of a little child.

It is not always possible to reform men by legislation, nor will legislation save the innocent and the ignorant from risking their all upon the airy promises of an irresponsible circular. But the time has come when legislation of a drastic character should be aimed at the 'bucket-shop' system as well as at the

'PROMOTER OF COMPANIES BUBBLE.'

And I hope that before long the Legislature will have the courage to take the matter up. It has often been said that, as a class, the clergy show a great fondness for Stock Exchange transactions, and I have heard more than once from stockbrokers that if there was any 'shady' transaction going, in which enormous profits were dangled before the eyes of the unwary, the readiest to fall into the trap were parsons and pious old ladies. I do not know why this should be so, but it is vouched for upon all sides. An outside broker once told me that in response to a circular which promised 'untold wealth in a week to anyone who would venture a few hundred pounds,' he received a letter from an old widow lady in a provincial town enclosing her *all* and expressing her belief that 'in answer to prayer she had been guided by God to make this investment.' 'Perhaps,' said the broker, 'you won't believe me, but I sent that money back. I felt that if by any piece of villainy I brought poverty and want upon that old widow I should deserve to be plunged into hell.'

Surely, if this incident shows nothing more, it reveals the fact that there was at least one who felt a twinge of conscience. But it shows more than that. It shows unmistakably that in the line indicated there is going on a species of organized and systematic villainy—a villainy which must be apparent to thousands of financiers in the City of London, a villainy which makes one's blood boil at the callous indifference of the gentleman at Whitehall who rejoices in the title of 'Public Prosecutor.' What *is* he about, that this evil goes on year after year unchecked?

But the gambling of the Stock Exchange and 'bucket-shops,' although appalling in itself, is as a drop in the ocean compared to that which is among us and eating into the very heart of society in the form of betting and wagering. There is no class of the community free from the pestilent plague of betting. From the highest to the lowest—the peer to the plough-boy, and the duke to the dustman—the vice claims victims, and wherever its vitiating influence is felt it is bad—hopelessly bad.

There is one very curious feature about betting, however, which ought to be mentioned. Nobody ever bets to win! So they say, at all events. And judged from the standpoint of those who bet, betting is a great object-lesson in self-denial and self-sacrifice, and ought therefore to be classed among the cardinal virtues. According to these, the 'backer' who puts *on* his 'crown,' his 'fiver,' or his 'pony,' would be most indignant if anyone made the suggestion that he had any desire to win or to take the cash of another without giving an adequate return. He does it, he says, to give him 'an interest in the race,' or a 'little pardonable excitement'—the great antidote to the monotonous routine of daily business. So when the day of the race, on which his money is staked, arrives, and purchasing his evening paper to see the 'result,' he finds that the horse he 'backed' has lost, *he rejoices!* He has had his reward in the excitement—that was all he sought—and he throws his cap in the air, glad that the other man will have the money! Now, doesn't he? Is not that typical of the ordinary man who bets? You know better! I know better! Experience among men, knowledge of human nature, the ordinary gift of common-sense, tells one that to lose money, however little, maddens a man, goads him on to still further ventures in the hope of recouping his losses, impoverishes his home, starves his wife and children, ruins his business, blasts his character, develops in him the most ignoble passions, and renders him unfit for the serious business of life. Is this indictment overcharged? You know it is not overcharged. Hardly a day passes by without recording a victim or victims. For every penny gained by betting upon the one side there is a corresponding misery and degradation upon the other side, and in any consideration of the subject the misery and degradation are factors which cannot be lost sight of. A man may plead, 'May I not do what I please with my own?' but the only answer to such a plea is, '*No;* you may not do what you like with your own if *what you like* brings misery upon other people.' Precisely the same argument might have been used, and doubtless was used, in defence of the slave-trade or concerning the inhuman traffic which floods our own streets to-day.

Well, this evil—this disease (for it is a disease)—of betting has assumed gigantic proportions, and as one views it to-day in all its manifold shapes, it seems almost hopeless to make any successful attack upon it. There have not been wanting men prominent in the sporting world who have denied the widespread nature of betting. Not long ago the editor of a sporting print—*The Pink'un*—set out to show that betting was on the decrease. How he must have laughed 'up his sleeve'! His attempt was a most dismal failure. Perhaps he was right in his claim that there are not now such large sums staked by individuals on single events as were staked formerly. But in that he appeals to a very limited number of people, and, after all, perhaps the real reason for it is the multiplication of race meetings, or, at the best, that a few men are not such *great* fools as they used to be in the good old sporting days gone by.

The evil has grown of late years, grown rapidly, until there is not a town, village, or hamlet in the land but feels its blighting influence. Nor is it difficult to account for its growth. Race meetings have multiplied within the past twenty years. The press has lent its aid to the movement, and given special facilities in every direction to men to bet. There are now many daily and weekly newspapers devoted entirely to sporting news—which, of course, means offering extra special help to the betting fraternity—whilst the ordinary newspapers, with only two or three exceptions, feel the force of competition, and confess themselves obliged to minister to the wants of the betting element. There is a demand, they say, and we must meet it with a supply, and, moreover, *it pays!* Then, again, the postal authorities have not shown themselves averse to offering, whenever possible, the means of telegraphic communication from race meetings and the like; and last, but not least, that great tribunal, Public Opinion, although generally believing the spirit of gambling to be wrong, has taken no decided stand against it. So, with these and many other facilities, the disease has spread and become a national scourge. Go where you will, you find it raising its hideous head, and wherever you find it, there you have developed to hand the very worst traits of human nature. And how far-reaching is the influence of betting! Now and again we get a glimpse through the medium of the law courts of what it leads to, but even there we gather really nothing of the widespread misery and ruin which it brings in its train. Men, women, and children are tainted with it. Take its effects in the City of London alone, and you will gather enough evil from it to make the angels weep. Where is the bank, or counting-house, or warehouse, or factory, or printing establishment, that is free from it? And most of these people find vent for their passion by betting on horse-racing. Not, surely, that they are deeply interested in the sport? Most of them may never have seen a racehorse nor would they be able to distinguish one from a draught-horse, nor do they attend race meetings. They gather their 'information' from touts and tipsters (who are invariably wrong), through the medium of the press. And the whole system is so ridiculous that it would be superfluous to stop and ask the *value* of the information given day by day, were it not that that information is implicitly relied upon by those to whom it is given. The editors of newspapers know full well that the whole thing is a miserable sham, that every day they are 'palming off' upon their readers several columns of matter which must inevitably have baneful results upon the community.

For saying all this, one is laughed at by men who consider themselves 'knowing,' 'sporting gentlemen,' 'men of the world,' and the like. A pack of fools—dangerous fools—on whom, for the benefit of our country, a strict watch ought to be kept. You may say this is rather hard coming from a parson, who cannot have seen much of the evil. But I know the atmosphere of which I am speaking, and I am not 'beating the air.' I know its baseness, its meanness, its cowardliness. I know how utterly impossible it is for any sign or form of goodness to flourish in its midst, and I assure you men that it is impossible to find a vocabulary strong enough in which to denounce it. The whole spirit of it is bad, whether it is in the form of betting, or in games of chance, or in a sweepstake or a raffle at a church bazaar —it is hopelessly bad. There can be no exception; the spirit of it is a wrong spirit, a spirit which degrades man and dishonours God.

But what are we to do? How can the evil be crushed? By legislation? By curtailing the freedom of the press? Englishmen shudder at the very thought of curbing the press, but surely it would be better that the press should be held by 'bit and bridle,' than that the moral tone of our country should be ruined, and we should become—which we are rapidly becoming—a nation of gamblers. Is it too much to hope that the vice shall be denounced from every pulpit in the land?

But here again we are met with varying counsels. Surely, it is pleaded, there is no harm in playing games for small 'points,' or in a raffle at a bazaar. And so the vice is not denounced; betting men sneer at the Church, and rightly so, for her half-heartedness. We turn, then, to Public Opinion. What can be done there? Among the upper classes, not much; the lower, still less. Yet one does not wish to give up the aristocracy, who have certainly mended their ways considerably with regard to drinking. Twenty years ago there was no harm seen in a gentleman getting dead drunk at dinner; to-day such an action would be considered the action of a cad. Cannot betting be so branded in society? Would to God that it could! That would be a great step. But it is not to the upper classes alone that we have to look so much as to the middle and working classes of the population. There is among these latter classes a gathering strength of brotherliness—a feeling which has its expression in the thought, '*I* am my brother's keeper.' It is to that growing spirit we must look for the formation of a public opinion upon the evil of betting and gambling which shall ultimately brand the scourge with that injustice and wrong which are its inherent qualities, and leave no effort unused until the evil be stamped out. With such a spirit we may demand legislation, and it will be forthcoming. May that spirit of brotherliness grow among us! for surely it is but a foretaste of the realization of the prayer—'Thy kingdom come.' Let me close by quoting the familiar lines of Leigh Hunt's poem, ' Abou Ben Adhem and the Angel':

> ' Abou Ben Adhem—may his tribe increase!—
> Awoke one night from a deep dream of peace,
> And saw, within the moonlight, in his room,
> Making it rich and like a lily in bloom,
> An angel writing in a book of gold.
> Exceeding peace had made Ben Adhem bold,
> And to the presence in the room he said,
> "What writest thou?" The vision raised its head,
> And, in a voice made all of sweet accord,
> Answered, "The names of those that love the Lord."
> "And is mine one?" said Abou. "Nay, not so,"
> Replied the angel. Abou spake more low,
> But cheerly still, and said: "I pray thee, then,
> Write me as one who loves his fellow-men."
> The angel wrote and vanished. The next night
> He came again with a great wakening light,
> And showed the names whom love of God had blest,
> And lo! Ben Adhem's name led all the rest.'

MARRIAGE LAW.

BY THE

REV. CANON H. SCOTT HOLLAND.

'*This is a great mystery; but I speak concerning Christ and the Church.*'—EPHES. v. 32.

IF we are ever tempted to suppose that the secular and the religious aspects of human life can be held apart in separate compartments, or that the Gospel of Jesus Christ makes its appeal only to the individual conscience, and has no positive bearing on social interests, our hopes of intellectual consistency are bound to come to an abrupt arrest at the point where we encounter marriage.

Marriage! Here, if anywhere, religion claims to be concerned. Always, in every place, form, and fashion, the religious instinct has fastened on marriage as its own. Round and about it the earliest memories of primitive faiths have inwoven their most intimate associations. Wherever we turn, at whatever age in the world's history, a nation's religion finds in marriage one of its pivot-points. Marriage can, of course, be secularized where religion is absent. But it is hardly possible, except under the influence of some abnormal reaction, such as overtook the early Reformation, for any living religious belief to exclude marriage from its sphere of action.

And, as this is obviously the case in the whole multitude and mass of human religions, so, again, our own Christian Faith, obeying the Divine inspiration of its Master's words, and guided by the earliest direction of Apostles themselves, assumed marriage as its own peculiar concern, and endowed it with its own authoritative sanction, and steeped it in its own spiritual temper, and veiled it in the light and music of its own innermost mystery, and filled it, and transfigured it, and established it, so that it became a wholly Christian thing, and, at last was so imbedded within the body of the Church that it became almost inconceivable that even its temporal, and legal, and external conditions could be separated from the special prerogative of ecclesiastical authority.

Yes, certainly, marriage must fall on to the religious side of our life, wherever our faith is in full play. And again, it certainly falls over on to the side of the individual conscience and the individual freedom of choice. Here in marriage, if anywhere, the inner world of feeling, of passion, of imagination, all that strange and delicate world which we would at all costs keep in our own possession, in its own sacred secrecy, unpublished, undisplayed, unadvertised, unhampered, must be intimately touched. We reach in marriage the very sanctuary where a soul puts out its claim to be itself and no other; to be hidden from alien eyes and unvexed by public supervision; to be at liberty to trust its private instincts and to develop its natural capacities. Marriage, then, engages all those innermost elements in us which go to constitute our personal and our religious individuality. That is certain.

And yet there is nothing which is more obviously and more essentially a public and social affair. Beyond all question the State must take account of it in all its bearings. The life of the whole community rests on it, revolves round it, springs from it. Far from being a merely private business, it has issues at every turn which compel the public legislation to take note of its every step, to follow its every movement, to inspect, to regulate, to direct, to guard, to license, to limit, to define, to handle it. Nor can it do this without a distinct conception of what it intends by marriage. For the matters which bring marriage under its handling, and which give to marriage its intense social significance, are no accidental incident, but belong to its very principle and purpose; and the State that is to be concerned so intimately and so minutely and so seriously with all the delicate details that grow up round and about marriage, must, perforce, have deliberately asked itself, what is its principle? what is its purpose? and must, as deliberately, have formulated an answer. The complicated legal mechanism by which a society controls and supervises the marriage of its citizens is bound to embody a definite ideal. It cannot be merely the formal and regulative action as of an indifferent spectator who has no other interest than that of keeping the peace.

Marriage is, then, the one absolutely inevitable point at which the theory of separating the outer and the inner order of things, the social and the individual life, the purpose of the State and the purpose of religion, must for ever break down. It cannot be done. Here the two halves must either collide or agree; they must have interests in common, interests that overlap, interests, too, that belong to what is deepest in each. A man or woman in marrying, however private, personal, intimate the motives that are at work within them; however profoundly to them it may seem to be their own affair, and no one else's; are, as a fact, undertaking of necessity public responsibilities which the entire body of their fellow-citizens are concerned in imposing, and are exercising the highest privileges of their corporate citizenship.

My brethren, you and I have come together here in St. Edmund's, just because we are anxiously inquiring whether our public and our private lives can be brought into harmonious agreement; whether our social and our individual consciences correspond; whether our conduct as citizens reflects in any degree the mind of Jesus Christ.

In such an inquiry, then, as I have tried to show, there can be no point at which the challenge rings out with sharper urgency, with a more piercing anxiety, than at this of marriage. And this urgency, this anxiety, are acutely heightened for us at the moment at which we stand, because the newer social ideals and motives which are beginning to tell upon our civic life, and to mould our legislation, have not yet shown what their action will be in this vital sphere. They have hardly yet displaced at all, in this department, those counter-ideas which everywhere else they are so rapidly ousting. Yet, at last, they are bound to invade this domain as well as all others; and when they do they will be liable to those peculiar perils which have always historically accompanied Socialism in its treatment of marriage.

These perils will be wholly different from those which have hitherto beset us. What have those been? What are they still? They are those which spring from Individualism; and from the Secularism which has been its outcome. Individualism has no consistent interpretation of marriage; for marriage is itself, in its very essence, the denial of Individualism. It asserts with all its force the incompleteness of the individual. It roots his being in partnership, in community, in corporate responsibility, in the intermingling of life with life. Individualism has no insight into such principles as these. For it, marriage can only be regarded from the point of view of the individual satisfaction gained in it; and its main anxiety lies in freeing this satisfaction from all unnecessary fetters. Its aim is to leave the individual alone as far as possible in making or unmaking his contract. Its legislation is all set towards loosening the ties as soon as they fret or curb the individual conscience. This convenience, understood in its full sense, constitutes the main ground of marriage; when it ceases, the justification for the contract is withdrawn, is gone. Hence the movement of Liberal, of progressive legislation has run so strongly for the last sixty years in the direction of free divorce. Of course there was the uncomfortable fact of children to be faced. This necessarily fixed some limitation to individual liberty; and, again, this involved public interests in securing that no social injury was incurred. For all this side Individualism, possessing, as it did, no ideal principle by which to bring together the personal satisfaction and the public obligations incurred by its indulgence, fell back on the protective and preventive action of physical science. It was inclined to suppose that medical knowledge could fix such regulations as were essential to the public well-being. The State must be guided by the doctor as to what it was bound to forbid. Apart from this, its whole object lay in securing perfect freedom to the contracting parties.

Liberty of contract, with medical science at hand to warn, and check, and advise, and relieve—here is the general picture of the situation, as the main mass of men who were concerned in making and administering the law have conceived it. And can we be the least surprised that, under the influence of such a picture, marriage became more and more secularized, in the narrow and worse sense of the word; and that, under the cover of such secularism, we should have terribly suffered from a wide invasion of practical methods by which the private satisfaction could be indulged without incurring any of the paramount and public obligations which tend to control, and to steady, and to moralize it?

Such an invasion could not but debase and disorganize the entire fabric of moral motives which sustain the purity and the honour of responsibility in marriage.

I thank God, from the depth of my heart, that, with the break-down of Secularism, we have made our escape out of the worst stress of the peril in which we stood. The individualistic creed, which supplied so much of the spirit which went to the justification of those methods, is, mercifully, fast vanishing away. And with it, too, disappears, I trust, a large body of those principles and motives which have for so long tended to the disintegration of social as well as married life, by interpreting freedom of contract solely from the point of view of the isolated individual. I cannot believe that we shall for long now continue to identify the advance of civilization with the loosening of the marriage law; or assume, instinctively, that progressive legislation lies always in the direction of facilitating divorce.

But, my brethren, these newer ideals that are so rapidly reorganizing our mental structure bring with them dangers of another kind. Ever since Plato sketched his wonderful Republic, it has been clear that the very fervour of an ideal belief in the unity of the social body might hasten and inspire an attack on marriage. 'Marriage,' 'The family,' 'The home'—these too often appear to such a belief to be the toughest obstacles against which it violently clashes. These, it fancies, are the final entrenchments behind which a stubborn Individualism obstinately resists. Safely laagered in this refuge, it refuses social assimilation. For Socialism, then, to leave marriage alone is to leave the foe in possession of all the fortresses which dominate the open country, which alone has yet been won. Nothing has been achieved so long as the corporate life of the community, with its common joys and common sorrows, its mutual responsibilities and mutual service, is blocked at the threshold of the home, within which, secreted and secure, the married pair laugh at the futile efforts to 'nationalize' a life which they intend to live to themselves alone.

So, again and again, the case has presented itself, and will present itself, to passionate Socialistic reformers; and this attack is all the more serious because it springs from what is highest and noblest in their creed. It is zeal for the full realization of brotherhood and of unity which tempts them to irritated violence against the obstructions that seem to bar advance.

Yet marriage and the home are, in reality, the very opposites of what such Socialism supposes. Far from being the true strongholds of Individualism, they are its exact antithesis. Marriage is the eternal declaration that human life is realized and perfected in community; in giving, not in taking; in service and surrender to another, not in self-regard, or self-culture, or self-isolation. In asserting this law as the prime necessity determining the continuance of the race, marriage roots the law in the innermost seat and principle of our being. It proclaims that law to be no accidental crown to our enjoyment. Rather, it is the basal verity without which we should not exist at all.

In marriage, therefore, lies the germ of the community, of the State—the germ of every claim by which it is made illogical and impossible for any one of us to imagine that he may live his life to himself alone. We belong to others by the mere fact of existing; and our own life becomes fertile, and realizes its fulness, only so far as it goes out from itself, and incorporates itself with another. This is the innermost truth of our being, which alone can interpret it, whether in the height of its spiritual aspirations, or in the length of its intellectual attainments, or in the breadth of its social enlargements, or in the depths of its fleshly instincts and motives. All through the finest fibres of the soul this one note rings out as the secret of the mystery—the note of a love that lives by giving itself away; and marriage is ever and always its concrete manifestation, its ineffaceable evidence, its unconquerable proof. Nor does the mystery so proclaimed arrest itself at man. Community of life, commingling of spirit, these are the hidden springs of that Divine intercourse, that sacrificial Blessedness which is the Eternal Godhead. 'God is Love.' 'This is a great mystery, but I speak concerning Christ and His Church.'

Now, if this be the heart of marriage, it can be only through some miserable blunder that it should be 'suspect' of Socialism. And what is the blunder? Is it not the old and familiar one of opposing the general to the particular? We fancy that in order to love all men more we must love each separate man less. We suppose that a strong personal affection for one must be in collision with the universal affection for all. But, in reality, if it is, it has falsified itself. The right way to love all men better is so to love one friend with all your heart and with all your soul, that in him you may learn to love every man who is in his likeness, and of his nature. An intense personal attachment is the training-ground in which we find out how wonderfully lovable a thing man is. If it be true to itself, it will act as an inspiration to prompt and kindle in us a tender kindliness for every man, woman, or child that we meet. The human race at large becomes tangible, actual, comprehensible, lovable in the face of him to whom our heart goes out in such abundance. If we fail to find our general sympathies widened by the intensity of a particular affection, we have somehow disturbed and hindered its own proper instinctive movements.

So with marriage. It is the ground of our corporate existence in society. It evokes within its own sphere the very temper of altruism, of mutual service, of incorporated interests, which has only got to be extended to become the true tone of the social citizen. And the way to extend it is, therefore, not to abolish the smaller sphere of its exercise, but, on the contrary, to fortify, to protect, to enrich, to intensify it. The closer and warmer the home affection, the larger and stronger should become those social instincts which make life inconceivable except in a community, and which constitute it a matter of sheer habit and of unmitigated joy to think always of others as well as one's self, to associate others with every word and work, to devote to the common welfare the richest energies with which man is endowed. Nowhere but in the home can these gifts be won. Their vigour will be proportionate to the fulness of the experience and of the encouragement which they have received through the happy opportunities of home. And if they stop short at the domestic limits, and refuse to open out to their wider office, they sin against the home as much as against the State.

All the motives, then, which make us keen to emphasize the enduring and paramount demands that the community should make on the individual's conscience; keen to urge upon the individual his responsibilities to the body corporate, and the moral need of heroic surrender to the public well-being; should force us to emphasize, with an equal anxiety and enthusiasm, the permanent and stable and responsible claims made over him by marriage. If the State is to be firm and high, so must marriage be, which is its fundamental discipline and school. If the State is to receive the light and inspiration of an Ideal, then marriage, too, must stand on Ideal grounds.

My brothers, what is the Ideal to be? That is the challenge which every year you will find driven home upon you with stronger and stronger insistence. You will be compelled to handle the marriage laws. The pressure of social forces is bound to require this of you. From all sides the pressure arrives. Sometimes from the side of what is noblest and finest in the modern movement, as, for instance, from the larger recognition of a woman's freedom and a woman's right. Sometimes, on the contrary, it will proceed from the terrible moral disintegration which is incident to a time of vast social change and of religious chaos.

Anyhow, it will come. And let me remind you, this law of marriage, which you will be compelled to touch and treat, has been taken wholly away from its ancient Ecclesiastical Administration, and committed to the Secular Parliament to direct, and to the Civil Courts to apply.

Quite rightly! I am not disputing this, or doubting its fitness. Only remember what that involves. Behind its old administration under ecclesiastical supervision, derived from canon law, there was always assumed a controlling and inspiring and sanctioning force, a fixed and unshaken authority—the Christian ideal of marriage. The law rested on this, beyond argument, beyond doubt.

Now, under its civil condition, under its secular administration, are you going to retain that ideal as your basis and your trust? Are you, or not? That is the question of questions! We have imagined for so long that by handing public affairs over to secular bodies to deal with, we shall avoid religious problems, that we have come to fancy that even the law of marriage, if so handed over, can be determined by plain common-sense and considerations of general expediency. But, as we started by saying, this vague supposition of a divorce between secular and religious interests, even if it can make a shift to manage most things, must be brought up short at this particular point. Marriage necessitates a positive ideal. And this ideal must have its base in the spiritual life. For, indeed, it lays such a tremendous strain on our powers of self-sacrifice for others, it involves such momentous responsibilities and such far-reaching issues, that nothing less than a spiritual ideal can have weight and authority enough to carry it through. Without this—if once it drops to the level of mere expediencies and utilities; if ever it be discussed, and handled, and legislated for, and administered on the materialistic grounds that are so inevitable to the average man of the world—it is bound to go under; it is bound to yield and break. The personal crises involved in its course are so intense, so manifold, and so severe, that nothing but an appeal to the spirit of self-sacrifice can carry men or women through them; and self-sacrifice can only be made at the altar of an authoritative or supreme ideal.

An ideal! We cannot be without it here! We cannot! And we dare not! for all round us, and within us, the hideous and awful powers of passion are waiting in the darkness for the opportunities offered by our indecision. Wherever we slacken in theory, or totter in will, or falter in insight, they press in, they rush forward, they seize the advantage, they gather to the onset. Hardly even at our best can we hold the fort of purity; hardly can we withstand the swarming hosts that even now are ever on the verge of victory. Let but one gate be opened, let but one wall be breached, and the day is lost.

How shall we stand? Under whose flag are we fighting? Is there treachery in the camp? or can we hold together, as one army under one Captain, that will die, but never surrender? The question is passing round from mouth to mouth—from soul to soul! The challenge is ringing in your ears to-day! A flag there must be, and a Captain whom we obey, or the ranks will sunder and fly. What is it? Who is He?

There is One who, as Son of man, claimed lordship over all that man is. There is One who flushed, at the marriage in Cana of Galilee, the water of human life with the rich wine of His own benediction. There is One who poured into the marriage union the strength and sanction of His own mysterious union with His Church.

He has endowed it with an ideal form by which it has withstood the incessant deterioration of lust, and has proved its power to survive the lapse of degradation, and to revive and to purify itself anew, and to establish itself, and to grow, and to show promise of yet finer issues to come.

That ideal has regulated hitherto all the main efforts of our civilization to secure, and govern, and liberate marriage. That ideal has yet much more work which it could do, in the way of demanding of man something approaching the self-sacrifice which marriage must always demand of women. It is for you and me, my brethren, to say whether it yet shall rule our inward thoughts, and guide our public actions. It is for you and me to nerve and brace ourselves to hold fast its law in voluntary obedience, even if it should come about that the conditions of a community which is now so largely non-Christian, should render it unfair and impossible to impose the full Christian ideal by law.

In any case we shall be sorely pressed! And we shall only have the strength to endure if we win it out of His own Name, who, however hard be the obedience He requires, will always, Himself, give us the grace to fulfil it.

RELIGIOUS EDUCATION.

BY THE

REV. G. W. GENT,

PRINCIPAL OF ST. MARK'S TRAINING COLLEGE, CHELSEA.

'*And He took a child, and set him
n the midst of them.*'—ST. MARK
x. 36.

I HAVE thought it well to take this text this morning, not because it suggests or is connected with any lesson as to the religious education of children, but because it may recall to us, in all that we to-day consider together, the constant remembrance which our Lord had of children, the constant likeness there would seem to have been before His mind between their innocence and the characteristics required of those who were to be worthy members of the kingdom of heaven. Those of you who are familiar with the Baptismal Service of the Church of England know how closely, in this matter, the Church has followed the example of her Master.

We shall all agree, doubtless, in some such definition of 'Religious Education' as this, that it is the teaching to a child of its duty in relation to God. That is to say, we shall teach the child to do right, because righteousness is the will of God; and to abstain from doing wrong, because wrong-doing is hateful to God. Yet with this we shall, for the child's own comfort, teach it also that God is slow to anger and merciful; that its natural childlike sorrow for having done wrong is acceptable in His sight; that it is possible with Him to begin afresh, and to make, in the future, some amendment for the sins of the past. And already, I would bid you notice, we are entering upon the circle of distinctively Christian ideas. We have come, I mean, within the range of that all but universal human instinct which cries out for a Mediator between God and man. If, that is to say, we are to have His will brought home to us under conditions which man can understand; if, conscious of the gulf which our sins set between God and us, we are to come to Him with confidence and hope; then we inevitably require, we unceasingly look for, one who shall represent God to us, and ourselves to God. So false is it, indeed, that either for the adult or the child the facts of Christ's history come first, and that upon them is then built the 'superstructure' of Christian ideas; so true that the child and the adult, and the child more than the adult, respond at once to the ideas, and find the greatest confirmation of the truth of the historical facts of Christ's life and death, in the supreme fact that these correspond to ideas so human and so universal that practically they may be called innate.

Thus, then, through this intimate correspondence between the heart and conscience of man, on one side, and the facts, historical and dogmatic, which Christianity alleges, on the other, we are brought face to face, at the outset, with what is the chief question of which I have to treat this morning: Are we to teach the great Christian dogmas to children? and if so, how in general are we to teach them? The mediatorship of Christ, for instance, with the two-fold truth which that involves of the Incarnation and the Atonement—are we to teach such doctrines to children, or are we to follow the way of those who tell us to teach simply the facts of Christ's earthly story, and leave them to discover later on in life the meaning which gives those facts their full significance?

1. This important question is often, as we all know, dealt

with in a very cavalier manner. 'These doctrines of which you speak,' it is said, 'are really matters of dogma; and the minds of children are not fitted to receive or to understand dogma; therefore dogma must be postponed.' Whether it be really true that the minds of children are unfitted to comprehend, at least, the practical scope of the great Christian dogmas is a point on which I shall have something to say presently. My immediate concern is with the implication contained in the remark which I have quoted, namely, that religious instruction can be given without the introduction of dogma. Surely, the thought of those who so speak is in subjection to a word rather than to the meaning of that word; they are so incensed at the word 'dogma' that they do not stop to ask themselves what, after all, the word means. Yet 'dogma' means nothing more at bottom than the statement in some form of words of what one believes to be true; and I would respectfully ask what teaching there is which is not, in some way or other, a stating of what one believes in words, and how anyone whose business it is to teach the young is to set out upon that work, if he be denied the use of compendiums and formularies? I know that it has been proposed to teach arithmetic without making children learn the multiplication table, and that some eccentric teachers would postpone telling a child that the earth goes round the sun until he is of an age to understand the reasoning on which that truth—always more amazing to children than any miracle—is founded. But the experience of practical teachers in all ages will be found, I believe, to confirm the common-sense view that you cannot teach everything to a child at once, but that it must begin by believing many things, even in mathematics and science, upon authority, before it can hope to establish them by independent inquiry. Yet this causing of children to learn, as true, statements which, from the nature of the case, they can only receive 'upon authority,' is of the very essence of 'dogmatic instruction'; and if my supposed opponent tells me that it is only in the religious sphere, and not in the secular, that he objects to such 'dogmatic instruction,' then, as I cannot but think, his plight is worse than before. For it is not easy to conceive of any religious instruction which does not begin by teaching the child that God exists; and this is a statement not only dogmatic in form, but dogmatic also in the fact that for children, as indeed for most adults, it comes and must come 'upon authority.'

2. Dogmatic instruction, then, at some point or other we cannot escape, either in religious or secular learning. Our opponents only come to grapple with us when they assert either that the dogmas we wish to teach are false—which is not a contention with which I have to deal this morning—or that they are incomprehensible to children, to which point I now return.

'Return,' I say, for I have already given it as my opinion that children are even more quick to understand the great ideas which the Christian scheme of redemption enshrines—the ideas of goodness, of transgression, of penitence, of forgiveness—than they are to be interested in the facts of our Lord's life upon earth as narrated in the Gospels. This is a point which I must leave, of course, to your own experience of children, or to your recollections of your own childhood; for my own part, I have never come across a child, and I do not believe it to be possible to come across a child, at least over the age of seven, to whom it is not only practicable, but easy, to give a well-comprehended idea of Christianity as a system of religion, and not merely as telling a beautiful story of Jesus of Nazareth. If this is not always the case, or if Christianity has sometimes been put before children in a perverted or unintelligible way, then, I say, this is not because those children have been taught the dogmas of Christianity instead of the simple facts, but because they have been taught the dogmas after a bad method. Children must be taught the dogmas of their religion

—as they must be taught everything else—after a method suited to the degree and capacity of their intelligence. Now, it is a well-known principle of the science of teaching —or, to use its hideous modern name, the science of pedagogy—that examples and illustrations shall precede, in any subject, the learning of the abstract rule which they embody; or, at least, that illustration and rule shall be in close contact with each other. Yet this principle, now universally recognised in secular instruction, is extraordinarily often forgotten by those whose duty it is to give a child an intelligible account of the main dogmas of religion. The child is set down to learn the Apostles' Creed or Catechism, says it by heart, and is then supposed to have received 'sound Church teaching'—as to which I can only say that it makes very little difference, in such a case, whether the 'Church teaching' is 'sound' or not; it will not last, because it will not have been brought into any sort of contact with the child's own experience. Every right rule of teaching is, in fact, reversed by teachers who thus hang the whole weight of their teaching upon the formulary; they are replacing the familiar illustration and concrete example, which children love, by the mere abstract statement which children are at such a loss to apply. Do I, then, for a moment deny the value of the abstract statement? No; but I say that, in order to have that value, it must be taught to children hand in hand with the concrete example and familiar experience which lights it up, partially if not wholly. You wish, for instance, to teach a child the doctrine of the Atonement. Then, if you are wise, you will begin by recalling to the child some experience of its own, in which another child interceded for it, or possibly bore part of its punishment. That child will understand you afterwards, when you go on to instruct it that Christ is the Mediator between God and men. If you cannot do this so easily with all Christian doctrines, you can at least do something of the kind with all of them. Believe me, a child to whom Christian doctrines have been made thus practically real, when it comes to the 'generalizing age,' the age of fourteen or fifteen, will recognise as familiar friends the more elaborately-stated truths which a fuller teaching will then put before it.

3. You thus see that, while I advocate that Christianity should be taught dogmatically from the earliest age—and, indeed, if it is not to be dogmatically taught, I do not see how it can be taught at all—I nevertheless hold that dogma should be taught to children after a different method from that in which it may be taught to adults—by the method, namely, of illustration and concrete example rather than by that of abstract statement. I believe this to be the natural, and therefore the most truly educational, manner of bringing children to an ultimate and intelligent acceptance of the great doctrines of their religion. But it is quite clear that if the method of religious education which I defend is to succeed, the same influence must preside over it from the beginning to the end—the teachers must be believers, and they must be religiously-minded men. They must be believers, because only a believer will be able to select and to treat the illustrations and examples, of which I have spoken, in such a way as to make them convincingly lead up to the dogmas or abstract statements of which they are meant to be the embodiment. I do not think this point needs labouring at. But, again, those who teach ought not only to be believers, but also religious men. True education, as we have begun to see even in secular learning, does not consist in the facts with which the memory is filled, or the rational principles with which the intellect is enlightened. All that may be done, and yet the child be turned out nothing better than a walking dictionary or an intellectual self-seeker. Education, in the highest or the deepest sense of that much abused word, means primarily this—the influence of character upon character. If it is true, as it indubitably is, that the character of the man who imparts their secular

instruction, and the mode in which he imparts it, will have a lasting influence upon the children who are taught, much more is it true that the character of the man who imparts to them religious instruction, and the mode in which he teaches this, will have a lasting influence upon the way in which the children conceive of religion. This point again needs no labouring. Only, I have said so much in order that we may remind ourselves that the best paper schemes of religious instruction can never work, unless we are also careful as to the hands in which we place the actual teaching.

I have been laying down leading principles; and in the consideration of them, my brethren, we have ascended to great heights. But here, at our feet, in the workaday world around us, there is controversy and strife; and I must say something of it.

It would indeed be unreal if, preaching on this subject, I were not to say a word on the struggle which is at this moment going on at the London School Board. Why, then, are Churchmen as a whole opposed to the School Board system of religious instruction? Let me premise in the first place that it is not out of mere jealousy of the Board schools. We should be well content to let the Board schools go their way, if the same measure of justice were dealt out to the religious instruction which is given in our schools as is rendered to that given in theirs. We have a most real grievance so long as the rates paid by Churchmen are taken to pay for undenominational religious instruction in which we do not believe, whilst at the same time we are compelled to tax ourselves in order to support the schools in which the Church instruction, in which we do believe, is given. But setting that on one side, why are we unable to accept for our children the religious instruction of the Board schools? I say no word against the teachers, who, to my knowledge, are in the main a body of Christian men, working hard and doing their best. But behind the teachers are the Boards who employ them; and what Churchman can be content with such a sliding scale of religious teaching as is revealed, when we compare, for instance, the religious syllabus of the Board of Birmingham with that of the School Board for London, or know that many members of the School Board for London itself are willing, and even anxious, to leave the Divinity of our Lord an open question? We have a deeper difficulty in the very character of the undenominational teaching itself. Such teaching may suit the great English Nonconformist bodies, which one and all make the real spiritual life of the individual begin when he has undergone some crisis of conversion or election, which may, indeed, occur at any time, but which is not usually expected to occur till after the period of childhood is over. I can understand why those who so believe think it enough if Bible facts alone, without Bible doctrines, are put before the minds of children. It is enough, in such a case, if the child be given the facts which, when the moment of conversion comes, will enable him to understand his emotions and profit by them. But the Church's standpoint in regard to children is wholly different. She regards them as already made members of Christ at their baptism in earliest infancy. She wants to remind them of that privilege and of the responsibility it involves. She wants them to understand that the work of Christ's redemption has already touched them; to tell them how they may come to God, without uncertainty, when they fall into temptation or sin; to show them the way of pardon and of new strength already open for them. She wants also to lead them on towards Confirmation, and to teach them something of sacramental grace. In a word, she cannot be content until to her own children she can teach the Church Catechism. And as none of these things are possible to her under the existing Board-school system, she cannot accept that system as a system of national education, unless and until, under it, there is possible for the Church children who attend Board schools an instruction in Christianity which is after a Church and not after a non-Church fashion. That is our whole case. We have no wish as a Church, as we certainly have no right as a Church, to hinder the State from giving to the children of England the excellent secular education which it rightly deems necessary in the primary schools. But we do respectfully demand that such primary education shall be given under such conditions as shall render it possible for Church children to receive, along with it, the definite religious instruction which their parents desire.

We make the demand in the name of Him whose representatives we are; we ask for the same liberty as our Master had; we claim also 'to take a child and set him in the midst of us.'

VAIN OBLATIONS.

BY THE

REV. T. C. FRY., D.D.,

HEADMASTER OF BERKHAMSTED SCHOOL, AUTHOR OF 'A SOCIAL POLICY FOR THE CHURCH.'

*'Bring no more vain oblations . . .
I cannot away with iniquity, and the
solemn meeting . . . Wash you, make
you clean.'*—ISAIAH i. 13·16.

THE Sermon on the Mount and the Public Health Acts—something of a contrast here! A Christian nation, with an Established Church, and a burning need for penalty on iniquity and neglect. 'Oblations made vain' by the presence of uncured evils that brand our profession with hypocrisy. The 'solemn meetings' of respectable parishioners at matins, and the iniquity of high rents for the slum-dwellings of great cities. These are surely the contrasts that Almighty God 'cannot away with.' In our ears, as in the ears of eighth century Judaism, should ring the prophet's warning cry: 'Wash you, make you clean.' At times we flatter ourselves at our progress, as we count up our Sanitary Acts; well, perhaps we might do so justly, if we called ourselves heathen still. But we confess allegiance to Christ; and He bid us deal with our neighbours as we would be dealt by. Just so, we say; that is the very reason why we pass Public Health Acts.

Let us hope so; but is that the reason why we *need* to pass them?

'Well, of course, there is so much sanitary ignorance. The poor are so prejudiced against open windows, and so unconscious of danger as to ashpits.'

Ignorance? ignorance of the poor? is *that* the only cause of our difficulty? is it to remove by object-lessons the ignorance of the poor that we have put penalties into the Acts? Undrained houses—you can enforce their drainage. If you are a person of some importance, gifted with a little courage and more obstinacy; if the inspector of nuisances is not first cousin to your landlord; if your Sanitary Authority esteem righteousness above rates, you may then positively enforce the drainage of your own or your neighbour's premises—after considerable strife. But did the ignorant poor build these undrained houses? do the people who live in them pocket their rents, own the leases, or benefit by the neighbouring clearances? Do the men who derive a profit from them profess a high standard of religion or of politics? do they profess Christ?

Cellar dwellings—oh, the Acts are very particular about them; they are careful enough to rule that they, too, must have drainage, and (what is more) proper areas and some light. How thoughtful! how Christian! how self-sacrificing! Is it, then, possible that, except for this law, by the pressure of legally-recoverable economic rent in a Christian land, human beings of our own nation, and possibly of our own faith, might be driven for shelter into holes in the ground?

Did this really happen before we actually rose to the level of this remarkable provision?

Streams, again, first amongst God's most beautiful gifts—streams cannot be polluted, the law says so; though some of us who know some English streams might not, on any less authority, believe it. Are they, then, turned into waterways of poison and death, because drains are dearer and will raise the rates? Some houses too, if unfit for human habitation, can (mostly after lawsuits) be pulled down; yet are they generally rented to the last hour of their accursed life.

And is all this the mere unfortunate result of ignorance of sanitary law? No, indeed; our Christian profession is a lie in the mouth of all who profit by this, or who are inert or indifferent about it. Christianity is the whitewash of the vestryman, the mill-owner, the cottage-owner—great or small—the selfish politician, the satisfied ratepayer, who either sees all this and says nothing, or grows fat upon its evils.

The two deadly foes of life and truth in this matter are greed and indifference. Indifference is greed's best ally. Indifference, with dull selfish eyes, from its coign of vantage, coldly watches the reformer's fall. '*I* live on the hill,' it says; 'why should I pay for my parish drains in the valley? *I* don't live over a sewer; thank God, *my* children do not sleep in a cellar. I only own a cellar to keep wine in; I don't need to let it for other people to sleep in. It is all very horrid, of course, but it is a question for law, for police, not for me. I do not wish to make needless enemies.'

But, my indifferent brother, greed has so drafted its laws as to suck its gains from your inertness. The law seldom knows compulsion; it is unworkable at times, when authority sleeps, except through some ratepayer like you. Have you no responsibility in the matter? Yes, depend upon it, the word is very near you: 'Inasmuch as ye did it not for the least of these My brethren, ye did it not for Me.'

'Well,' you say, 'I do not wish to be inert. I should like to do something. But the question is so vast. How am I to begin?'

'Vast,' yes; it is on that word that the man with vested interest relies. At each municipal election, that would sweep out his Augean stable, if the broom could be got into the right hands, he confuses the issue. He alarms the conscientious. He arouses the bigot. He allies himself with the wirepuller. He bribes the needy or the drunken. He flatters the partisan. So he wins, and the evil goes on.

'What can you do?' Realize your own personal responsibility as part of the social organism. See clearly the moral claims of cleanliness, fit dwellings, pure water, streams free from poison. See how the stunted soul is cribbed within the stunted body in the City slum; see how disease and death grow out of the miasma that you need not live near. 'It does not touch *your* homes.' No! but that only deepens your debt to the community. Some of the men and women in those overcrowded tenements, those airless cellars, those undrained streets, are actually producing for *you* (in the complex interaction of social conditions) the margin of profit or economy that has drained *your* house or has kept the roses in *your* children's cheeks.

We send our anarchists to the guillotine, but why do we not realize that we may be ourselves creating, or at least permitting, the very conditions which breed the discontent out of which the anarchist makes his converts? And if our own conditions raise us beyond the reach of any such hopeless propaganda, do we realize why God has granted them to us? Is it not to arouse us to the very worth and need of the great crusade, on behalf of the less happy? Go home to-night, then, and plan at once an active union of a few resolute friends, who shall do for your own neighbourhood, or for some less favoured quarter, what Mr. Horsley—to his lasting honour—has done for the 'Dusthole' at Woolwich. Make it your ambition, for Christ's sake, to count up the number of unfit dwellings you have helped to close, of cellars you have emptied, of streets you have drained, of pure supplies of water you have seen given. Or go down to the Oxford House in Bethnal Green and in evenings won from personal pleasure help those who are fighting like evils in various ways. Or send us some of your superfluous money to the White Cross League in Dean's Yard, where month by month we meet, and out of a failing exchequer strive to bring home to men's consciousness the intimate connection between housing and immorality; and our exchequer fails, because immorality, though it blights our land, is 'really so difficult to mention.' The Bishops do not know how to make their clergy take the whole question up; and the clergy are often quite sure that it is wisest to keep silence about it; and the men of Clubland run away as soon as the subject ceases to be *risqué* and brings home God's judgment to the conscience; and it must not be named plainly in West-End Churches, for fear of offence. Yet if every man who reads this were to send us ten shillings to-night, we could do such a work in this mission as we have never yet been able to do.

Can you do all this and make no enemies? No, you are sure to make enemies.

Rejoice, when in the cause of sanitary homes you are ill spoken of, or even persecuted, by the Scribes and Pharisees of modern life, the men who whiten the sepulchre in which lies buried their neighbours' well-being and their own eternal hope. For the real root of these evils is greed—greed battening on defenceless lives; greed defying law; greed prospering on the degradation of the poor. If ever you engage in a sanitary fight, you will find in it a clearer revelation of the base in human nature than in almost any other conflict. Oh! can there be amongst Christians to-day anyone who ever pockets one shilling for the neglect of needs like these? anyone who cares not, so long as he gets his rent, to ask how his rent is earned or is deserved? Then, may God have mercy on his soul! for drink, disease, decay, handed on by heredity to another generation, thrive and breed and prosper herein. The casual worker is thus degraded; the unemployed is thus manufactured. The very future of English labour, then, rests on the enforcement of sanitary laws. Expose, therefore, the hypocrisy of the religious rack-renter; expose the lack of patriotism in the indifferent.

How many an infidel is created by such evils, who shall say? Can we do less than wonder at the supreme patience of the poor, to whom, though they be her own children, England at the present price of City land cannot give the shelter a stepmother might not grudge the least valued and the least loved?

Economy? By all means let us have economy, if it means less luxury, less waste, less indulgence; but not an economy that defeats itself, that breeds heathen, that degrades labour, that bleeds chastity to death.

This hateful gospel of 'getting on,' bred of *laissez-faire* economics and men's selfishness; this craving after wealth; this rule of the successful usurer; this 'rem, quo cunque modo rem'; this competition in pleasure, is like a serpent winding its slimy coils round the strong limbs of England. At one end of our social gradient we have the fortune-hunter, who has forgotten to be a founder; at the other, the undersized, the under-fed, the over-tempted, the sweated, and the workless.

On whom does it depend whether these things can be altered? On you and on me—on us, with ears to hear and eyes to see. Some changes in the law, in themselves slight, would do much. Let us demand from our legislators the extension to all England of Ritchie's Metropolitan Act of 1891; let us make medical officers of health and inspectors of nuisances irremovable, save with consent of the Local Government Board; let us grade, pay, and promote them for good work done; let us extend to England the Irish Labourers Acts; let us write *must* for *may* in all sanitary legislation; let us increase our inspectors; let fines be large enough to deter. Let us give to candidates for our division the option between these changes and the loss of our votes.

But let us also, with clean hands ourselves, set to work to create a higher Church tone upon these matters. Let us put pressure from such changed tone upon our leaders, especially our ecclesiastical leaders, to trust the English people rather than the London vestries; to push forward sanitary legislation in quarters whither God has sent them on purpose—legislation in which for the jerry-builder and the slum-owner there shall be no possibility of contracting out.

A united Episcopate, that dared to originate some proposals on City-betterment or on a municipal death-duty, if only by way of hint to a Ministry, and to suggest the earmarking of funds thus obtained, that they might only be used for housing the poor, might fearlessly face a few worthless epigrams even from peers, strong in the love and gratitude of a wider brotherhood amongst suffering populations.

But let us not forget ourselves. 'Me, me adsum qui feci.' Our tone it is that has made this possible. Why and for whom have we voted? For doing or for not doing what have we criticised the Home Office or any other authority? Has it not seemed to us as if Lent had only a message of penitence for the neglect of some spiritual duty, and no bearing upon claims such as these? That is not the teaching of theology, if its Canon still includes the Jewish prophets. That is not the teaching of the Gospel, if the lesson of the Gadarene demoniac has still a meaning for the world.

There they are, our demoniacs, amongst the tombs of an insanitary life, possessed with the devils of disease, degradation, and impurity; the chains of law, and even of respectability, they rend; really, no well-to-do person can always safely pass that way. They are an offence unto us.

And Christ is on our shores, too—the Christ we profess to follow. We may be freed from our devils if we will; but we must pay the cost.

We can have our outcasts back, clothed by a living wage, and in their right mind for culture and faith; but we must surrender our swine.

If, for the sake of the human hope for our fellows, we cannot forego our comfort, our time, much less the dirty money our pigs bring us; if we must have, even at this cost, the ground-rent of our slums, the margin that comes to us out of ruinous contracts and sweated wages and high rents, Christ tells us plainly that we are no followers of His, say we 'Lord, Lord,' as loud as we may.

'What shall we do, men of this wealthiest of the world's cities? Shall we give our swine to save our fellows, or shall we with one consent entreat the Christ 'to depart out of our coasts'?

RECREATION.

BY THE

HON. AND REV. E. LYTTLETON,
HEADMASTER OF HAILEYBURY.

'*Whether therefore ye eat, or drink, or whatsoever ye do, do all to the glory of God.*'—1 COR. x. 31.

THE subject of this morning's sermon is a very wide one, and I therefore make no apology for plunging at once into it. What is recreation? is our first question. Secondly, How far is the true idea of recreation being observed at the present time? Thirdly, Is there anything we can do?

I. A moment's reflection will convince us that many of the prevailing notions about recreation fall very far short of the meaning of the word itself. There is a strange and striking dignity of idea in this word. We men never dare think of ourselves as creators of anything, however much we may flatter ourselves on our skill in fashioning and working with a given material. But for a large portion of our lives we speak of ourselves as re-creating, or bringing into being something which has been spent. That which we re-create is spent energy; and the power of doing this is one of the most precious of those with which we have been endowed, and yet, in the common notions on the subject there is much that is trivial and very little that is dignified. People talk and think of recreation as if it meant simply bodily exercise, or absolute inertia, or some empty pastime. But if the word really means bringing into life again energies that are failing, surely it points to something higher than this.

Recreation depends on the compound character of men's being. We consist of body, mind, and spirit, and the simple fact is that the true well-being of these three constituents depends on the harmonious employment of all three in due succession and in orderly proportion. In its highest sense recreation is not rest, except in the sense in which that word is applied to God's unceasing, unhasting energy of action; but it is a change of activity. Unless there has been a violation of natural laws, the best way to recruit the mind is to exercise the body. This, I take it, we all recognise; but we are less alive to the fact that the best way to recruit the body is to employ the mind. Still less do we clearly perceive that the truest recreation of both body and mind is to exercise the spirit. You will say, perhaps, that when a man is thoroughly tired out in body or mind he cannot employ other faculties, or, if he does, the effort is injurious. But I answer that this is an indication of excess which requires artificial treatment, and is a violation of the laws of harmonious activity. If recreation must take the form of inertia, or pure idling, it is a sign of disease. If the mind, for instance, is so exhausted that the powers of the body are for the time paralyzed, no doubt there has been overstraining. Our bodies ought never to be so tired that we cannot use our brains; and neither body nor brain should demand such complete inactivity as to forbid us to lift up our thoughts in prayer. True rest is a change of activity. How has the statesman who is just now retiring after sixty years of unparalleled expenditure of energy, how has he maintained the well-being of bodily and mental faculties through all these years? By a constant succession of variations of activity. There is the secret! Man is not meant to be a creature of one activity. That is why our religion consists of a combination of faith and works. That is why the character of our Blessed Lord manifested such a wonderful blending of the active and the contemplative life—patient and prolonged expenditure of energy alternating with the solitary hours on the Galilean hills. People often talk with enthusiasm about the simple creed of Christianity being the imitation of the character of Christ. If it be so, at least let us recognise this double element, and try our best not to deprive our social or political or philanthropic energy of the unspeakably precious recreation of spiritual communion with the Most High.

II. So much, then, for the principle of recreation. The Anglo-Saxons have been forward in giving it prominence in the national life. Our idea of recreation has been a narrow one, and far too much identified with bodily exercise. But still it has played, and is playing, a very important part in our development. What, then, has been the origin and motive power of our national games?

Perhaps I should be rash in attempting to give a very positive answer. It is well known that through the influence of the Puritans, a large number of national and popular games were extinguished during the seventeenth and eighteenth centuries, and it seems as if there were some close connection between the revival of games and the rise of our great industrial system. The first set of rules for the game of cricket dates from 1774, just five years after Watt took out his patent for the steam-engine, and belonging to the same decade as that in which our domestic system was transformed into a factory system by Hargreaves, Arkwright, and Crompton. Does it not look as if the increasing industrial toil led our energetic operatives to find the needful recreation in outdoor games? We must not be too sure. Cricket, for many a long year, was mainly confined to the youth of the upper classes; but still we should not forget that, during the stimulus of competition and the feverish energy of work which have marked the last thirty years, we have witnessed the rise, growth and popularization of football. Surely this was a healthy symptom! Surely the introduction of this excellent form of recreation deserved to be welcomed, as a sign that there was still life and vigour in England?

But, alas! it is against the best institutions and agencies that Satan puts forth his greatest strength. The tendency of good things to degenerate is the saddest feature in social life. Let us look closely at some of the causes of decay of our great English game.

It has not been necessary for anything violent to be done. If, as I believe, the corruption of what is best is the work of our watchful spiritual enemy, he had a pattern before him to guide him in his work, and show him where the poison could be instilled with most effect. You have heard enough, and perhaps more than enough, of the corruption of our industrial system. Certain it is that there are vast evils connected with it—interlaced with it, and so incorporated with it that the best men are well-nigh in despair of a remedy. I don't wish to dwell on these, but to remind you of the cause. Something has worked secretly and silently through all these years and gone far to spoil a grand fabric of English enterprise and energy. What is it?—because we find exactly the same cause is now working havoc with our national games. Whatever it is let us recognise it, and not be afraid to call it by its true name—for its true name is 'covetousness.'

To make clear what I mean by degeneracy, let us contrast the two following pictures. The first refers to cricket as it was played in many parts of the country some twenty-five or thirty years ago. A club was formed, including men of all classes of society—the sons of the squire, the parson, the local gentry, the shopkeepers, the clerks in the village, the gardeners and men-servants from the wealthier houses. On most evenings in the week there was practice on the ground in the squire's park, where in all friendliness these different members of society gathered together in thoroughly healthy play; and their unity was still further cemented by the good spirit evoked in the weekly matches. Keen rivalry without bitterness, honest effort, unselfishness, manly endurance of failure, insight into others' claims—all these qualities were directly encouraged by such recreation as this; and I doubt if any amusement so thoroughly beneficial to all concerned could be found in any form of recreation known to the civilized world. Now, this has not wholly died out yet. But let us contrast it with the other picture, representing an Association football match in the north of England. A club has been formed in a big town. How? Not by local energy and love of the native country district, but by a company with a keen eye to profit. Everything depends, therefore, on the gate-money, as it is known that with sufficient inducements 20,000 or 30,000 people can be gathered together and pay so much a head to see an exciting football match. But to make it exciting the play must be first-rate, and what matter if the players have no connection whatever with the locality? The players are only important as bearing on the question of spectators. So agents are sent far and wide, mostly into Scotland, to secure recruits to supplement the local talent if there is any. Sometimes, it appears, every single man in the team is an importation. From eighteen to twenty-eight years of age, these young fellows are paid enormous wages; if successful, they can command their own price, and, so far from having any interest in the particular district to which they have been allured, their chief anxiety is to let it be known that they are willing to transfer themselves to any other club or company that will offer higher wages than they are now receiving. This goes on till the prime of their youth is past, and they are turned out into the world unfit to learn any trade, and almost certain to be burdens on their country as long as they live. And among the spectators—so far has the English instinct for fair play suffered in the prevailing frenzy—it has, I am told, again and again happened that the life of a referee at the end of a match is hardly safe from the mob of disappointed loafers who have put their money on the losing side, and are ready for any violence against him, though they know he has only done his duty.

This is a sad and sorry sight, my friends; and yet even Association football was for a few years, between 1870 and 1880, played in much the same spirit and with the same good effects as village cricket. Its name has not always been the mockery that it now is.

Now, what are the chief characteristics of these two forms of so-called recreation? The first did good in many ways, but its chief and most admirable characteristic was the spirit of *brotherliness*.

And the other? The other does harm in many ways, but its chief characteristic is the spirit of *estrangement*. There is no evoking of local patriotism; there is no concord between the managers and the rank and file; there is suspicion, born of greed, and smouldering animosities, because everybody who is connected with the arrangements and the play is bent on making money.

But we must consider some collateral and less direct effects of this state of things. So vast and widespread an organization is certain to tell in many subtle ways on the tone of society. First, there is the mischief that looking-on is substituted for bodily exercise. We have no right to talk of national games unless we mean games that are played by the people of the nation; but we are drifting to a state of things when the games will only be national because Englishmen look at them, and those who play them are paid £200 or £300 a year for doing so. Paid players and vast hordes of idle spectators—these were symptoms of the decline of Rome; but we have a feature to add peculiar to ourselves—our spectators come together by the thousand for betting. And then I would have you remember that the unhealthy excitement caused by these public displays goes far to corrupt the tone wherever football is played. Such a glamour is thrown round it that it has become a doubtful question among some energetic young town clergy whether they ought to encourage their lads to form a club among themselves, the truth being that as soon as they give themselves to a game so infected with spurious excitement and feverish rivalry, they can think and talk of nothing else. This means that the mischief spreads from the centres of excitement and corrupts the outlying districts, where there was, at least, a hope that the game might be played in its primitive simplicity.

But there is one baneful effect of this state of things less obvious than those I have mentioned, but well worth considering—I mean its effect on the tone of the public press. Consider the problem set before newspaper editors. To make a living for them, the paper must sell, and, in presence of fierce competition, it soon becomes recognised that pence must flow in without too much attention being paid as to the quarter whence they come. What the average mass of people require, that they must have, or the sale dwindles. Now, what do average people require? We will think of the way a working man spends his leisure. In the afternoon he witnesses an exciting football match; in the evening, if he has the chance, he goes to a political meeting—all the more readily if he thinks the speaking will be of the vituperative kind. The following morning he buys a daily paper which professes to discuss all sorts of difficult and complex questions relating to public affairs. Is it not certain that his appetite by this time has been quickened and stimulated in the direction of a craving for excitement, so that if by chance he comes across some impartial and well-balanced decisions in the paper he finds them intolerably dull? He is learning, not only to feed himself on excitement, but on that special form of excitement which comes from being a spectator of a conflict; and his natural propensity to be a partisan has been so much encouraged that life without conflict is to him a poor and tame affair.

Hence the peculiarly modern development of abusiveness

in politics and abusiveness in the public press. A newspaper must not only take a side, but must take it violently; and to anyone who knows anything of the atmosphere that surrounds football matches, especially in the North of England, it will not appear a fanciful or far-fetched inference to say that this woeful eagerness to witness sharp conflict is materially quickened by the prevalence of these violent athletic contests in which a score of paid men play and 20,000 look on, imbibing, surely, all the mischief and none of the benefits that belong to modern athleticism. If there are any here who think that acute party spirit, and the desire to treat politics as if they were a game between two sides, are favourable symptoms of modern social life, they may be content to acquiesce in modern developments of football. But those who do not may surely trust that some healing influence is at hand to save the tone of English public life, and with it a grand English game.

I do not deny that there would be some justification for calling this a needlessly sombre picture. But the gloom of it is relieved by enough light to let us perceive one great and encouraging fact—the presence of law. It is a violation of the law of brotherliness which has wrought the sad effects we know so well in the commercial world; and the same violation of the same law is producing the same effects in athletics. Let us take heart in the thought that this lesson is one which it is not yet too late for us to learn. We need discipline before we can grasp large and unfamiliar truths, and now is the time for us to take note that the time of discipline is at hand—'the axe is being laid at the root of the trees.' Is there anything, then, that we can do?

III. First, we can give a hearty support to the managers of the Rugby Union, who are doing their utmost to stem the rising tide of professionalism—not as men who are merely consulting a passing convenience, but as those who in a gallant and unpretending way are doing something to keep alive the true idea of recreation. That is one thing. But as regards the whole question, it is painfully and abundantly evident that we have here a disquieting symptom of a deep-seated social evil.

To lop off a dead branch from a precious tree is better than nothing, but it is not the same thing as curing a disease at the roots. Covetousness is at the root of this decaying branch of our English oak; and to cure a deep-seated evil your remedies must go deep and begin early. Men of business can, if they choose, train up their sons to look upon money as a trust, and not as a possession, because the first condition of brotherliness is that those who have should know themselves as stewards. And if you choose, you can do more than this; you can inspire them by your own example with a true view of the meaning of life and of the recreation of spent energies. God has placed us here not to become wholly absorbed in a complex commercial machine of our own fabrication, nor to give all we have to the building up of a muscular body, but to learn the great mystery that bodies are the temples of mind and spirit, and not only are as wonderful in structure, but are also immortal in their destiny; and for those reasons, and those only, are they to be jealously guarded, harmoniously developed, and lovingly adapted to the spiritual service of our Incarnate Master, Jesus Christ.

THE IMPERIAL CHRIST, AND HIS DEMOCRATIC CREED.

BY THE

VERY REV. C. W. STUBBS,

DEAN OF ELY, AUTHOR OF 'CHRIST AND DEMOCRACY,' ETC

I. Town Problems.

'And many, hearing Jesus, were astonished, saying, Is not this the carpenter? . . . And Pilate said unto Jesus, Art Thou a king then?'
—St. Mark vi. 3, and St. John xviii. 37.

A CARPENTER or a king? Which was He? A workman or a leader of men? Let us think!

The Divine Founder of our religion, the great Head of our Church, is known in the sacred records, and has been designated from time to time in the long history of Christian society by many names and many titles.

Is there any true sense in which it is right for you and me, without irreverence, to speak of Jesus Christ as the greatest of social emancipators, the most potent of labour leaders? I think so.

Every king and leader of men is enshrined for us in his own age. Indeed, you will always find, I think, that the best history of any age is to be found in the biography of its hero or greatest man.

The golden age of classic Greece you will better understand if you think of it as the age of Pericles; the majesty of imperial Rome when you think of it as the age of Augustus; the era of Italian Renaissance when you connect it with the thought of Leonardo da Vinci, Michael Angelo or Raphael; the epoch of the Protestant Reformation when you speak of it as the times of Luther and Erasmus, and Colet and More.

But when we come to speak of the King of the kings of men, the *Flos Regum Arturus* of the heroes of humanity, of what special age is He the measure? The Christ has for His times all times. Not the first century only, nor the second, nor the twelfth, nor the sixteenth, nor the nineteenth, is the age of Christ. 'The present days are His days, and we are His contemporaries.'

VARYING PICTURES OF THE CHRIST.

But when we try to picture His personality, how do we think of Him? Have we—you and I, Churchmen of the nineteenth century—any different picture of the Christ in our imaginations than the Christians of the first century, or the fifth, or the twelfth?

It would be strange if we had not. For certainly, not only the strictly theological, but the imaginative conception of the personality of the Christ has varied greatly from age to age. You can see that that is so nowhere more vividly than in the history of Christian art.

As you gaze upon the earliest Christian pictures in the Roman catacombs, you cannot fail to recognise that the conception of Christ which was conveyed to the simple minds of the men of the second and third century by the gay and winsome figure of the Good Shepherd, with the happy sheep nestling on His shoulder, with the pastoral pipes in His hand, blooming in mortal youth, must be very different to that of the men of a later age, for whom the gracious and gentle Pastor has given place to the crucified Sufferer, depicted in countless aspects of misery and woe, from the gaunt and ghastly Crucifixes and Pietas and Entombments of the early Florentines, to the sublime dignities of Michael Angelo and Tintoret and Coreggio.

Nor, again, can you help feeling that the conceptions of Christ's personality conveyed to the Italian Churchmen of the Middle Ages by the numberless pictures of the Madonna and Child, unfailing in their sweet and gentle lessons of the divinity of childhood and of mother's love, must be far different to that conveyed to the Flemish Christians of the fourteenth century by such a picture as the Van Eycks' 'Worship of the Immaculate Lamb,' with its sublime figure of the omnipotent Christ, the King in glory, enthroned and crowned, with hands outstretched in royal priestly benediction of the world.

Now, looked at from this point of view, what should you say was the special aspect of the person of Christ most characteristic of our age? Fifty years ago I think it would have been difficult to decide.

THE DIVINE COMRADE.

But to-day I think there can be no doubt that, largely due to the more directly historical interest awakened by various foreign studies of Christ's life from a merely biographical point of view, and largely inspired in our own country and Church, I do not hesitate to say, by the spiritual beauty of the figure of Christ as represented by the Unitarian Christian, Dr. Channing, and still more largely perhaps by the conception of the office and character of Christ as the federal Head of humanity, the King and Consummator of society, and of the doctrine of the Incarnation as the consecration of all human life, instilled into the whole of modern theology by my own revered Cambridge teacher, Frederick Denison Maurice, we have learned to worship a more human Christ—kingly and Divine still, it is true — commanding our reverence and devotion and humility, but still full of human friendliness and sympathy and love—a Divine comrade, not

> 'Too bright and good for human nature's daily food,'

ever ready to help and guide us through the endless moral perplexities of everyday commonplace existence, ever ready also to illuminate for us with some far-reaching principle the difficult modern problems of history and politics and science, of poetry and art, of trade and labour.

Am I right in adding those last words? Is there any modern reading in these days of industrial war, competitive industry and of an economic system,

> 'Where faster and faster our iron master,
> The thing we are made for, ever drives,
> Bids us grind treasure and fashion pleasure
> For other hopes and other lives'—

is there any modern reading, I say, in such days of the Christ message, 'Come unto Me, all ye that *labour*'? Is the Christ really 'the same yesterday, to-day, and for ever'?

Let us go back and feel once more, if we can, the significance of that life manifested in Nazareth all those years ago.

THE DEMOCRATIC NOTE OF THE GOSPEL.

There is no fact, my friends, more removed from controversy than this, that Christianity arose out of the common people, and was intended in their interest. When Christ came, He came as a poor man in the outward rank of an artisan. He was a true child of the people. In the very Song of Praise which burst forth from His mother's lips, when she knew that of her was the Christ to be born, the democratic note is first sounded which has echoed on through the history of the Church.

THE BIRTH-SONG OF DEMOCRACY.

You and I are so familiar with the words of the *Magnificat*, as we sing them day by day at evensong in our Churches, that in all probability we miss the significance of that note. But when the Church, evening after evening, all through the parishes of Christendom, is singing this hymn, she is unconsciously foretelling—the most ignorant and prejudiced of her priests are foretelling—that greatest of all evolutions, which the Mother of Jesus saw to be involved in the birth and work of Christ. To Mary, at that moment of inspiration in which her lips poured forth this birth-song of democracy, was revealed the stupendous reversal, political and social, which the birth of the Son of God, as the Son of man, as the Son of a poor carpenter's wife, was bound sooner or later to produce in all the world.

You will find that same democratic note, the note of social passion, struck by the Son of that same socialist mother and carpenter's wife, when in the full blush of manhood He stood for the first time face to face with his brother men in the synagogue of Nazareth:

> 'The spirit of the Lord is upon Me,
> Because He anointed Me to preach the Gospel to the poor:
> He hath sent Me to proclaim release to the captives,
> And recovery of sight to the blind,
> To set at liberty them that are bruised,
> To proclaim the acceptable year of the Lord.'

No wonder that the common people heard Him gladly, and listened with delight to the gracious words that proceeded out of His mouth.

It would have been strange had they not done so, when we remember how completely such doctrine seemed to satisfy the popular ideal. Of all histories, the history of the Israelites is the one, notwithstanding the outward form of their national constitution, in which the democratic spirit most constantly predominates. No tribunes of the people had ever been so bold as the prophets of Israel. They were, in fact, the champions of popular liberty and popular justice at a time when those virtues met with little regard from either priests or kings. The thought that God was the Protector of the poor, and the Avenger of the oppressed, was to be found in every page of their writings. When, therefore, Christ stood up for the first time to speak to the people, He could not well find words more clearly expressing the popular hope and longing, than those which he quoted from the great statesman-prophet of His country.

True, His after-teaching and life must have seemed as little short of mockery to those whose passionate enthusiasm for the redemption of Israel centred in the expectation of a militant and world-conquering Christ. When, for example, in the Sermon on the Mount, He ascribed the heroic character to those citizens of His kingdom who were not proud and rich, valiant and strong, but meek-hearted, self-controlled, peacemakers, childlike, innocent, simple, His teaching must have come as a chilling disappointment to the popular hopes of His day; yet in reality, if you will think of it, that Sermon did in reality contain the Popular Charter of the world's liberties, did inaugurate as vast a revolution as the world has ever known; for beneath those Beatitudes of the New Kingdom Christ had placed a principle which proved itself not only the most powerful solvent of ancient civilization, but also the great motive force in the progressive social order of the present.

THE MOTHER-IDEA OF CHRISTIAN CIVILIZATION.

It is the contention, indeed, of those who accept the Christian philosophy of history as the true one, that the struggle for liberty in its various forms which has in effect been the subject of the civil history of modern Europe since the time of Christ, is directly to be traced to the primary Christian doctrine of the intrinsic value of the human soul as such. That, it may be said, is a spiritual idea. True, but it is a spiritual idea which easily bears translation into a political one.

And, as a matter of fact, that is exactly what did happen. We have no time now to enter upon the historical retrospect that would make that plain.

SLAVERY AND PATERNAL DESPOTISM.

You have only to think, however, of the revolutionary force which Christianity exerted on the civil order of the ancient world, not only in its effect on the institution of slavery, upon which the civil order of Greece and Rome was economically based, but also its mitigation and final abolition of the despotism of paternal power, which was the dominant idea in the family life of Græco-Roman civilization, to see how far-reaching has been that principle.

It is quite possible that there may be those in this church who will think that I am hazarding a bold pretension when I claim the abolition of slavery as a Christian achievement.

Well, I am quite aware that slavery lasted in Europe down to the thirteenth century, and that it is the fashion in these days to contend that slavery perished owing to purely secular causes—the 'march of intellect,' the discoveries of science, the utilization of steam power, the natural rise in the standard of comfort, and so forth.

But, my friends, can you honestly think so? The march of intellect indeed! Why, the race that gave birth to Plato, Socrates, Aristotle, Sophocles, Phidias, Euclid, Archimedes, and Ptolemy could not even conceive of a state of society where slavery should not exist. Civilization appeared to them to require the servitude of the masses as its necessary foundation.

It was not cruelty or callousness that prompted Aristotle to divide 'tools' into two classes, 'living' and 'lifeless,' and to place 'slaves' in the first class. It was not want of intellect; *it was want of faith in human nature.*

CHRIST THE SLAVE OF HUMANITY.

'Who would do the scullion work in the great household of humanity if there were no slaves?'

This was the question that perplexed the great philosophers of antiquity. This was the question which Christ answered by making Himself the slave of mankind and classing Himself among the scullions. It was not the 'teaching' so much as the 'doing' and the 'being.' The spirit that dictated the words, 'Even as the Son of man came not to be ministered unto, but to minister, and to give His life a ransom for many,' dictated also, do not forget it, the death upon the cross. It is that spirit which has destroyed slavery in every Christian land; it is that spirit which will establish one day a true social order upon earth—a kingdom of heaven on earth, in which 'Christ shall be all and in all.'

'THE MILLS OF GOD GRIND SLOWLY.'

True, the spirit of Christ has never yet been fully obeyed, or even understood by all His followers; but upon the day in which it is obeyed, in which it is understood, life on earth will be life in heaven. But, my friends, you must not expect everything in eighteen hundred years. Astronomy, geology, biology, are three voices which all remind us that the hand of God works slowly. The student of evolution tells us that it took several hundreds of thousands of centuries to change a beast into a man; it may well take as many centuries to change earth into heaven, the kingdom of man into the kingdom of God and His Christ.

CHARACTER OF CHRIST'S LEADERSHIP.

But meanwhile it is important for you and me that we should be on the right track. And for myself I know of no better way of assuring ourselves of that than by taking care that we are treading in the footsteps of the Divine workman of Nazareth. Jesus Christ must be our Leader. But we must not misunderstand the character of His leadership.

NOT A CONSTITUTION-MONGER.

Jesus Christ will not furnish us with any ready-made scheme for a new and perfect human society. He is a social emancipator. Yes, but not a politician, not a constitution-monger, not even in the strict sense a legislator. You may go to His teaching for principles, for seed-thoughts, for inspiring motives, but you will find nothing there to hamper free human growth, for God has supplied men with faculties to frame social institutions for themselves, and Christ will leave these faculties free to work. He will emancipate, but He will not compel. He has left no authoritative precedents in regard to things which men can manage for themselves. For He knew that it is not possible to walk by the letter and by faith at the same time. The true Christian society was to be ruled not by a fixed code of particular rules, but by an indwelling spirit. The Christian disciples of all ages were to regard their Master's example as a sacred rule, but they were to go to the record of His words and deeds, not as to a civil statute-book where they might expect to find the ethical difficulties of all time scheduled and codified, but they were to go to it as to a well-spring of spiritual influence, where they might imbue themselves 'with the same mind that was in Him,' and let their own behaviour afterwards flow freely from it.

'SOMETHING MORE' THAN ACTS OF PARLIAMENT.

My friends, when sanitation, and education, and science, and political reform, and socialistic legislation, and the organization of labour, have all done their best and failed, as they all undoubtedly will fail, unless *something more* is also added, then I trust that we shall all of us, whether rich or poor, capitalist or labourer, begin to find out what that *something more* is. Then we shall begin to perceive that, after all, it is not new Acts of Parliament that are needed, Employers' Liability Bills, Boards of Arbitration and Conciliation, Labour Bureaux, an eight-hours working day, but a new spirit, a spirit of mutual concession in both individuals and classes, a spirit of frank justice on the part of both capitalist and workman, recognising that the loss of one cannot be the gain of another in the unity of the one life, a spirit of love, and self-control, and self-sacrifice as apparent in the life of the Family, of the Class, of the Nation, of the Church, as in the life of Jesus of Nazareth.

CHRISTIAN-SOCIALISM OR SOCIAL-CHRISTIANISM.

That spirit, and that alone, as I believe, will enable us to apply our knowledge and our wills to settle Land questions, Church questions, Labour questions, to address ourselves steadily to the work of Christianizing Socialism, or Socializing Christianism (I care not how you phrase it), of honouring and encouraging, of consecrating, of nationalizing the labour classes, while never unwisely pampering them; of dishonouring and discouraging and denationalizing the idle classes, and never ignorantly establishing and endowing them, teaching them that as the Divine Workman of Nazareth was subject to law, so must they be subject to law; that as He bore suffering for the good of His brother men, so must they be prepared to suffer and to serve for their comrades and fellows.

THE WORKMAN'S COMRADE-KING.

Ah, friends, to this we come at last, that all depends on knowing Christ more perfectly! And *that* we shall never do until we have all learnt to cast out that spirit of Antichrist which, while admitting Christ's Divinity, denies His Humanity, and have learnt to throw ourselves in perfect trust and faith on Him, whose whole life and character is the witness for the ultimate supremacy of love over all human society. We must learn—as I said at the outset—to realize the human Christ, the Carpenter of Nazareth, the great Companion, ever ready to bestow His friendship where it is most needed, ever the Emancipator of the captive and the oppressed, the Champion of the wronged, of the fallen, of the guilty, of the victims of Pharisaism and hypocrisy and greed and passion; the Friendly Christ, who had a heart for the poor, and wanted to turn the world upside down, but did not expect to do it in a day or a year, but was satisfied to go, apparently, a long way round to do it, but intended to do it at last and conquer.

This then, my friends, or something like it, is the imaginative conception of the Personality of the Christ that we want; at least, this is the Christ, as it seems to me, which the English workman wants, and at any rate of this I am certain, that he at least will never consent to accept Jesus Christ as the true Son of God until he has first learnt to realize Him as a true Son of Man.

And further than this, I am sure that we shall never persuade the labour classes of this country, alienated as, alas! in too large a degree they are from recognised Church influences, to accept this conception of Christ, as Saviour, Leader and King, or, indeed, any conception of Christ worthy of the name of Saviour at all, whether personal or social, until they see that we, the professed followers of Christ, Churchmen as we call ourselves, whether Conformist or Nonconformist, are prepared to put our Church creed into touch with our daily secular life, the life of Trade, Commerce, Politics.

They will say to us—and rightly say to us—' You may stand up in your churches week by week, day by day, and publicly and solemnly confess your Church's Creed, handed down to you from a long antiquity; but what we want to know is this, Are you willing to read into that Creed these clauses which we seem to think you ought to have learnt from the Spirit of the Christ of To-Day?'

THE DEMOCRATIC CREED OF THE CHURCH.

1. We believe that in all the disputes and conflicts, industrial, social, political, which rend the body politic of this Christian State to-day, the prime necessity is frank Justice between class and class.

2. We believe that the first principle of Christian Justice

is this, that the loss of one cannot on the whole be the gain of another in the unity of the one life.

3. We believe that the first principle of Christian Liberty is this—freedom, not to do what one likes, but freedom to do what one ought, and that therefore respect for individual rights should never blind us to the higher reverence which we owe to social duty.

4. We believe that the first principle of Christian Equality is not equality of distribution, but equality of consideration, which may be expressed in the maxim that every man is to count for one, and no man for more than one.

5. We believe that the first principle of Christian Fraternity is that 'we are all one man in Christ,' and that no man can say sincerely, 'Our brothers who are on earth,' who has not previously learnt to say, 'Our Father which art in heaven.'

6. We believe that the competition of trade has been assimilated to the competition of war, and stands condemned by the assimilation.

7. We believe that in Christ's kingdom the law of life is service, not competition, and that no money, therefore, is legitimately earned which is not an exchange value for actual services rendered—services which minister to life and help on the common good — and that consequently no wealth is honest which is accumulated by taking advantage of the weakness or the ignorance of our neighbours, and rendering them no equivalent in reciprocal service.

8. We believe that society exists not for the sake of private property, but private property for the sake of society.

9. We believe that the right use of property must be insisted upon as a religious duty; that as capital arises from common labour, so in justice it should be made to minister to common wants.

10. We believe that wealth does not release the rich man from his obligation to work, but only enables him to do unpaid work for society; the only difference, indeed, accord-

ing to Christian ethics, between the rich man and the poor man seeming to be this—that the poor man receives his wages at the end of the week, and does not get them unless his work is first done; whereas the wealthy man receives his wages first, and is bound as a matter of honour to earn them afterwards.

11. We believe that it is not the equalization of capital that is needed, but its moralization.

12. We believe that as all life is of the kingdom of God, and the Church of Christ is concerned in the ways of His disciples, however secular they may seem to be, it is the duty of the Christian citizen to build up, as far as his influence extends, the life of the great civic brotherhood to which he belongs, and of every sphere of action which it contains in justice, righteousness, and the fear of God.

13. We believe, therefore, that it is the duty of the Christian city, in the interests of its citizens, to provide, first, for the three essentials of physical life—pure air, pure water, pure food; and, secondly, for the three essentials of spiritual life—admiration, hope and love; and with these objects in view, we believe that such a city will take legal measures to prevent the pollution of air, water, food; will preserve open spaces and town gardens; will provide playing-fields and gymnasiums and baths in connection with all elementary public schools; will pass, not only a Sunday Closing Act for public-houses, but a Sunday Opening Act for public libraries, museums, art galleries, and other drawing-rooms of the people.

14. We believe that in such a city the citizens will have full control over the regulation and license of all trade, and that the drink traffic as at present organized, standing condemned by Christian principle, will, if not suppressed altogether, be very largely curtailed, and in the meantime, compelled to compensate the ratepayers of the city for the increase of poor rate and police rate directly traceable to its influence.

15. We believe that in any truly Christian city there would undoubtedly be a by-law of the Council suppressing the scandalous indecencies of the Divorce Court, and the brutalizing horrors of the Police Courts in the public prints, and prohibiting the publication in any newspaper of all betting lists, the odds on sporting events, and any information likely to stimulate gambling, whether on the Turf or the Stock Exchange.

16. We believe that the conception of family life is not only human, but Divine, and that, therefore, it is the duty of the Church of Christ to unite men in actively opposing the corruption of national and social life, which springs from neglect of the principle that personal purity is of universal obligation upon man and woman alike; and, when necessary, to co-operate with the civil and municipal authorities in police efforts for the repression of prostitution and the degradation of women and children.

17. We believe, finally, that Christ's whole earthly life is a direct command to His Church to spend a large part of her time and energy in fighting against all circumstances and conditions of living which foster disease and hinder health; in delivering people from evil environment and fatal heredity; that, in fact, the whole secular history of the Church should be an endeavour to realize in act the daily petition of her dominical prayer, ' Father ! Thy kingdom come. Thy will be done, *on earth !*'

II. Village Problems.

'And Jesus gave them authority . . . and sent them forth to preach the Gospel of the kingdom of God . . . and they departed, and went throughout the villages preaching and healing everywhere.'—ST. LUKE ix. 2-6.

I SPOKE to you yesterday of one aspect of the doctrine of the Supremacy of Christ in human life. I tried to suggest to your imaginations such a picture of Christ's Personality as should not seem to be out of harmony with a conception of Him as the greatest of Social Emancipators, the most potent of Labour Leaders.

It was not, of course, that I do not recognise that Christ was more than this; that His Supremacy meant more than the supremacy of principle in the realm of Social Politics or Labour Ethics. It must indeed be of the essence of any true faith in Jesus, of any vital belief in the doctrine of the Pre-incarnate Word and the Incarnate Christ, that He should be recognised as Supreme over all realms of thought or action—history, philosophy, ethics, art, poetry, trade politics, science—and that it is in consequence of that claim that the moral character, no less than the intellectual attitude of every one of His baptized disciples, should be affected and influenced by His Spirit.

For what does that doctrine of Christ's Supremacy, of Christ's Kinghood, whether we regard the question from the point of view on the one hand of Evolution, or on the other of the Incarnation, imply?

It means, in the first place—does it not?—that God has a plan for the world; it means that order and progress in human civilization is real; it means that the cry of the cynic and the social agnostic—

> 'Fill the can, and fill the cup,
>   All the windy ways of men
> Are but dust that rises up,
>   And is lightly laid again :
> Drink to lofty hopes that cool
>   Visions of a Perfect State:
> Drink we last the Public Pool,
>   Frantic love and frantic hate—'

is not only not true, but is a gross blasphemy against God's purpose for humanity; it means that God has for the world a great educational plan, by which both the perfection of the individual and the perfection of the race is to be accomplished; it means that in the development of that plan each age of the world has its own special work to do; it means that progress is not only a vital fact of human existence, but that it is its vital law; it means that there *is* a Christian ideal for society, that there *is* a social order which is the best, and that towards this order the world is gradually moving; it means that Christ, as the Eternal Word of God, has always been, and is still, the acting organ of creation and Providence, ever operating in the region behind phenomena, the originating cause of all energy, all life, all thought; it means that Christ, 'in becoming incarnate, did not desert the rest of His creation,' but is the quickening impulse of all that is best in what we call modern civilization, the nourisher of new graces in the ever-widening circles of the Family, the Society, the State, the inspirer of art and literature and morals and government, by lifting them all into a higher atmosphere of hopefulness, of faith in the ideal, than was ever possible until He came, 'the Head over all things to the Church, the Fulness of Him which filleth all in all.'

That is the aspect of Christian faith, at any rate, which in the opinion of the Social Union, which has projected this course of special Lenten sermons, there seems a special need to press upon the consciences of the Christian community at the present day. It is this aspect of the faith which inspires the three great rules of our Union, and which prompts the demand we make upon each one of our members to be ready:

1. To claim for the Christian law the ultimate authority to rule social practice.

2. To study in common how to apply the moral truths and principles of Christianity to the social and economical difficulties of the present time.

3. To present Christ in practical life as the living Master and King, the enemy of wrong and selfishness, the power of righteousness and love.

No one, I think, can doubt that much progress has been made during the last ten or twenty years in 'preaching this Gospel of the kingdom,' in bringing home to the hearts of the people that the message of Jesus Christ, the mission of His Church to the present age, is a social message, a social mission.

But much yet remains to be done; and nowhere more, I think, is this social mission of Christ's Church necessary than in the country parishes of England. There is no class of men in the country—and I speak what I know, for I have been a country parson myself, and have lived among them for nearly twenty years—more self-sacrificing, more earnest-minded, more generous-hearted, taken as a whole, than the rural clergy of the Church of England; and yet one may be pardoned, I think, if sometimes one ventures to doubt whether they all quite sufficiently appreciate the width and largeness of the mission of preaching and healing which is committed to them as priests of the Church of Christ. I wish sometimes they would read with wider eyes the words of their priestly commission, 'Take thou authority to preach the Word of God, and to administer the Holy Sacraments in the congregation'—in the light of the original commission of Christ to the Twelve—'He gave them authority . . . and sent them forth to preach the Gospel of the kingdom . . . and they departed and went throughout the villages preaching and healing everywhere.'

For we are being asked, and rightly asked, as the result of the great democratic movement of our day, What sign is there in the Village Life of the England of to-day that the priests of Christ's Church are awake to all the meaning of the Gospel of the kingdom? What have they done? What are they doing to make the English villager feel that Christ is the true King of the village—that the Christ principle must be supreme in the realm of Village Ethics, of Village Politics, of Village Economics? Personal independence, mutual responsibility, the rights of liberty, the duties of association—these are all root principles of the Gospel of the kingdom; these are also the essential qualities of the English character in the earliest time of which history has anything to tell us.

Are these the principles of English village government to-day? Are these the essential qualities of the English villager as we know him to-day? If they are not, who is most to blame for that? If they are, why then all this timidity, this want of faith in the sturdiness of national character, in the average common-sense, even, of the community, which seems to me to have characterized too many Churchmen in the discussion, both in and out of Parliament, of the provisions of the Local Government Bill?

This is not the place, of course, to enter into any partisan political discussion of that measure. But let me ask you for a moment to consider one attitude of the critics of that measure which hardly suggests any point of party politics.

It is continually said, it has been said over and over again to me in country parsonages during this last year or so: 'Do not imagine that I am opposed to village councils in themselves. I quite recognise that village government does need revision; but it is so important that that government should be in the hands of the best men, and what I fear is that the councils will be dominated, not by the best men, but by the most talkative—the local preachers, the unionist agitators, the noisy, vulgar, pot-house politicians, and that, in fact, the best men will retire from public life in disgust, and a consequent deterioration of national character in the country districts set in.'

That point of view was put in a more statesmanlike way by one of our greatest authorities on Local Government, an M.P. for a Northern county, in the *Times* a few weeks ago. He pointed out that when once the Bill had become law, and had passed out of the region of acute Parliamentary discussion, then and thereafter nothing in the whole domain of local government would at all approach in importance, as regards the daily life of the population, to the question, How are these local councils exercising the power which Parliament has given them? Are they acting not only with zeal and honesty, but with wisdom and economy in execution? In short, do they sufficiently command and obtain the services of those men in each parish and district who are by their ability, character, and experience most competent to judge for what objects their own and their neighbour's money should be spent, and when that is settled to spend it with the utmost economy and advantage?

These, no doubt, are sensible and wise questions, but when this authority goes on to contend that, with a view of securing that the best men of the land-owning and the leisured class should have a direct inducement to interest themselves in local administration, they should have a limited but assured representation on the local councils, I cannot but think his suggestion unworthy and unstatesmanlike.

For, surely, if such men are 'the best men,' the true aristocracy of rural life, they will do their duty without such inducement; nay, further, I do not hesitate to say that such men, *if they be the best men*, whether squires or parsons, will be little short of abject fools if they do not lead the village life of the future, as they have done in the past.

But in the future they must *be* the best men, and they must set the lead in all that makes for goodness and wholesomeness and righteousness in village life; they must realize the vast importance of the revivification of village life at which this Local Government Bill at least aims.

And to do that they will have to face, as it seems to me, these three questions, and somehow find an answer to them:

I. Can we do anything, by the help of the provisions of this Act, to increase the general pleasantness and attractiveness of village life in England?

II. Can we do anything to improve the economic condition of the rural labourer, and thereby to raise permanently the standard of comfort and joy of his class?

III. Can we do anything to quicken citizenship, the sense of public responsibility and civic duty on the part of the English villager?

I. As to the attractiveness of village life. Village life is dull. In winter time, especially, the hearth of the village ale-shop is too often the only social centre of warmth and light and colour—and of much also, I fear, which is only not dull because it is wicked. What does the average villager know of the pleasures of books, of pictures, of music, of art, of conversation, of all, in fact, that makes the social life of the classes above him glad and bright? What does he know, even, of rational, intelligent pleasure in the sights and sounds of the country life about him, of the spiritual joy of earth?

> 'The moving glory of the heavens, their pomp and pageantry,
> Flame in his shadowed face; but no soul comes up to see.
> He sees no angels lean to him, he feels no spirit hand,
> Melodious beauty sings to him—he cannot understand.'

And yet, surely, he ought to know something of the pleasure which God intended that beautiful things should give him. He ought not to be satisfied—at any rate, we ought not to be satisfied for him — with only labour and sleep and feeding. When the work is done, and the sleep is over, and the eating is finished, shall not the man himself presently wake up, and find his spirit afterward an hungered, and know that it lives not by bread alone?

If those, who claim to be 'the best men' in every village community will only ask such questions as these, What shall we do to make village life a little less colourless and sad? How shall we break its monotony and commonplace with some stimulant which shall not be vicious, with some pleasure which shall not be merely gross and sensual?—I think they ought to welcome the advent of this Bill, and cheerfully undertake to see those of its provisions which deal with the Public Libraries Act, the Baths and Washhouses Act, the acquiring of public recreation grounds and walks and the building of parish halls, put as rapidly as may be into effect.

II. With regard to the economic conditions of village life.

I will not enlarge upon this point. But I think those provisions of the Bill which speak of the acquisition of land for allotment purposes, and which deal with the question of setting the Small Holdings Act of 1892 to work, ought at least to suggest to our village 'best men' such questions as these:

1. Does the English State consider that production of food for the people is the primary charge on the land, and with that object in view does she desire to retain a rural population of workers on the soil?

2. Does the English Church consider that national character is of far greater importance than national wealth, and from that point of view is she prepared to welcome the revival of an English yeoman class as one of the surest means of building up a sturdy, wholesome, pious national character?

And if they answer those two questions in the affirmative, this question must immediately follow:

3. What is the legitimate economic ideal of the English peasant of the future to be?

Until these questions are settled it is quite useless to go further.

What, for example, is the use of all these various and conflicting schemes of the technical training committees of the County Councils up and down the country, if we have not first made up our minds as to the special object of all our training? The peasant proprietor or small farmer of the future—if we decide that the creation of such a class is to be our national aim—will need a very different training to that of the wage-earning farm hand of the present: for small farming, remember, is practically a lost art in the greater part of England.

III. Lastly, how can we quicken the citizenship of the English village? How shall we give the spirit of local patriotism, the sense of civic duty, to our village communities?

I confess, as a clergyman of the Church of England, as a country parson for very nearly twenty years, I am somewhat ashamed to put this question. For I cannot forget that there was a time in the history of the Church of England when she played no unimportant part in the development of popular liberty. It was in the Parish Vestry of old times that the two great principles of English free institutions—the principle of mutual responsibility and the principle of personal representation—were most surely nourished in the heart of the English citizen. The Parish was, in fact, the truest school of Politics, for there men learnt, in the active business of responsible life, those primary lessons in public justice and self-government, in public discussion and social duty, which go to form the character of a capable citizen.

I would to God that even at this last hour the authoritative leaders in our Church would throw aside their timid counsels, their grudging policies, their half-hearted aspirations, and would welcome with generous-hearted trustfulness this demand of the rural population of England to take part in the nation's work, and would exhibit some at least of the democratic faith of earlier days, when at the wreck of Roman civilization the Christian Church learnt to build up, by means of the Teutonic spirit of individual freedom and social fidelity, a new and higher order of civilization. I would to God that Churchmen of to-day could be made to understand, that our bishops especially could be made to understand, that faith in democracy does mean, for the true Christian, faith in human progress, a conviction little, if at all, short of religion itself, that the impulse which is hurrying the world on to new destinies is but God's appointed means of leading His children one step nearer to the solution of that great educational problem which He has set them of making His kingdom on earth, as far as possible, a likeness of that which is in heaven.

I would to God that every country parson at least might learn to welcome this Bill heartily, for sure I am that any Churchman who is earnest and honest in his desire to raise the moral condition of his fellow-countrymen, who desires to forward any true measures of civic well-being, for the administration of village justice and prevention of wrong-doing, for the safety and security of person and property, for the well-ordering of poor relief, of education in its widest sense, of public health and public wealth and public wisdom; who would promote the growth of a hearty sympathy between class and class, a right appreciation of the mutual obligations and relations of each, and a cheerful and happy fulfilment of what those obligations and relations bring to each, will recognise that one of the surest methods lies in the revival of the good old English principle of self-government in the village 'moot' or council, and its foundation on a sound representative, democratic, and therefore Christian, basis.

And now I must conclude. It has been my object to impress upon you as Churchmen the lesson that, if the Church of Christ in this country is to fulfil her Master's mission, she must set herself to the task, both in the towns and in the villages, of solving the great problem of the reconciliation of the classes, of the developing and the harmonizing of all the elements which go to make a wholesome national character.

Will this generation, do you think, see the problem solved?

If we had only faith, it might be done to-morrow. We have the living Christ with us, and all that we need is not to resist His Incarnation in and through us.

What an achievement it would be—the crown of the century—one more upward step gained in the path of social evolution 'towards the perfect man, the measure of the stature of the fulness of Christ!'

DRIVING THE GOLDEN SPIKE.

I have read that when the great Pacific Railroad was completed across America, the event was made memorable by driving a spike of gold where the last rail joined the track which had approached from either side of the continent. The Evolution of Humanity has been marked at well-defined points of progress by similar golden spikes. What a trophy for Christ our King, if the close of the nineteenth century of His era could be marked by the solution of this problem of Labour and Capital! Let us pray for it, let us work for it.

> 'Strike the golden spike, master workman, on the way,
> Humanity is travelling with the travelling of the day.
> Strike the spike of gold! as struck primeval man
> When a highway Godward to travel he began:
> When with celt of unhewn stone he scored the birth of mind,
> And the first milestone was set that left the brute behind.
> Strike! strike! master workman, on the road to kinglier men;
> Scarce the spike is driven ere thou must strike again:
> For the road thou buildest is a road without an end,
> Leading where with human effort hope and reason blend.
> Through the heart of elder evil, the love of brutish strife,
> Drive the spike of human progress and a loftier, truer life.
> Gird the world. The nations blend. Peace and love proclaim;
> To evolve a nobler man is the world's predestined aim.'

COMMON-SENSE IN RELIGION.

BY THE

VEN. ARCHDEACON WILSON.

THE subject upon which I have to address you is 'Common-sense in Religion,' its need, its dangers, its limitations. My main difficulty will be to dispose of certain common-places quickly enough to leave time to get to the heart of the matter.

Religion in one person calls up ceremony, or it may suggest asceticisms, needing some restraining element, which we call common-sense, to check exaggerations. There is, however, a wisdom not of this world, which has a deeper insight into the secret springs of religion, and not only common-sense. It was common-sense which sat on the bench when Festus cried with a loud voice, 'Paul, thou art beside thyself.' Common-sense, if it is candid, will admit that the underlying forces of the world have always had to be joined with what deemed itself common-sense. Common-sense will distrust itself in judging of ideals, for fear that it may be insensibility to the highest in man.

Religion in another will suggest another train of thought. There is a large educational, parochial work to be done. Much of such work is done by the clergy, because more qualified laymen offer no help. The world is divided into those who do something, and those who look on and say it might be done better. I would respectfully suggest to that sort of common-sense that so to look on is very mean. We cannot have too much common-sense. The children of light may well be as wise as the children of this world.

Again, the phrase suggests the higher aspect of our work. Christendom is agreed that we are bound to bring all the world to the knowledge and love and imitation of Christ; and yet often the differences and rivalries of religious bodies are an insult to common-sense. Why these quarrels—this distrust? Is there no function for common-sense in relation to religious bodies? There is room for common-sense to understand better our relations with our fellow-Christians. We need to get beyond sects and parties, and be rivals only in good works.

This use of the phrase suggests another: these differences are all caused by varying opinions. Is there no room in this department of religion, known as dogmatic theology, for common-sense? What has common-sense to say to the various theological systems that have arisen in the Church or have departed from it? Theologies and creeds have been so elaborate, and so fine have been the inferences, and compacted into systems with such wonderful precision—schemes of salvation, theories of sacraments, ecclesiasticism, and the like, that common-sense stands aghast, and asks, Is there no place for me here?

What shall we say? There is need enough, but we must be clear what it is there is need of. The problems of human existence can never cease to attract men's minds. Say what we will of theology, it exercises an irresistible attraction. There the soul seeks her home; there man rises above materialism; and it is inevitable that men, absorbed in such a study, should state their own inferences and system, and try to impose them upon others.

What is the function of common-sense? It is to recognise the want of a corrective to the exaggerated notion of completeness that belongs to every system, and declare that we know in part.

Common-sense has taught us that theology can never

with safety get far from the original intuitions. No inference that does not rest upon the Word of God, and find its echo in the hearts of men, can be trusted as universal truth. But danger lies here also: if a man without spiritual mindedness, without the habit of prayer and meditation, without humility and transparency of mind that comes only with an awakened conscience, and relying upon his business capacity, dares to pronounce upon the aspirations of the soul for God, he is sure to be wrong.

There is an intuitive power in all pure minds in relation to God in those regions of thought which are called spiritual.

Common-sense is right in distrusting a cold and unfeeling theology. The other day a demagogue, who ought to know better, talked to working men of the rot of the Church of England Prayer-book. Was that common-sense? These men would revise the Psalms, Isaiah, and even the words of Jesus Christ Himself. This is common dulness, and want of any common-sense.

Common-sense in religion suggests to some of us, if we are men, an inchoate self-conscious form of spiritual force that fills the universe. There seems to be a common instinct pervading all men, which is no other than the Spirit of God Himself. Below our ignorance, and selfishness, and sins of every kind, buried deep below, lies the Spirit of our Father. It is like the internal heat of the earth, flaming out in the volcano here and there in fire and warm springs, and never wanting where you go deep enough.

This sanctified, Divine common-sense, this Spirit of God in man, is not scattered among and separable like grains of gold in sand, it is diffused everywhere in human nature. He who thinks of man in this light can never for a moment think he can live to himself.

The Divine education of the world will be his aim. He will be very humble, and he will think that he is a mere unit in the universe. The experience and the mysteries of redemption, the incarnation, eternal life, duty to God, will be to him terms of mystery with an unknown element in them. He will show a reverence to God, remembering that He is in heaven and we on earth. So his words will be few. Such common-sense as this—so deep, so strong—will develop into the wisdom that turns to scorn all extremes, and will dare to tell the truth, though hated by priests and demagogues, as only priests and demagogues can hate the light and truth. It will seek the praise of God, and love Him and his fellow-man.

Lastly, it is this universal sensibility in man to the highest ideals that makes us feel that Christ is in very truth the Son of God. We claim Him as the perfect embodiment of the Divine Spirit in which we share. We bow before Him as the Son of God, and make Him a leader of men into the presence of His Father. And therefore this common-sense in religion, this universal sensibility in man to the highest ideals, so far as we share in it the aim of religion, is to be Christlike, to help men to be good and do good.

In purity and kindness, duty and courtesy, lies the field of religion. Common-sense will apply religion, therefore, to common life, to trade, to all social actions. It repudiates that religion lies between man and God as his maker, and sees it is only half a truth; but that it lies between man and man also as his brother. Common-sense that has no such outcome will not be the religion of Jesus Christ. May God grant that we may have more of this kind of sanctified common-sense! Amen.

SOCIAL HOPE.

BY THE

REV. PREBENDARY EYTON,

RECTOR OF HOLY TRINITY, UPPER CHELSEA.

'*Many there be that say, Who will show us any good?*'—PSALM iv. 6.

IT is always a comfort, when we are depressed and downhearted at the outlook around us, to find that there have been men in other days who have had to pass through our own experience. There was in David's day a good deal of pessimism flying about like some foul disease—a good deal of wholesale and thoughtless depreciation both of things generally and of man and his condition; there were men then who deliberately declared life to be a woe and a curse, not worth living, who criticised everything, not with a view to bettering it, but with a view to cheapening it and making it out to be worthless.

There are such men in every age, who live to damp and depress our spirits: a walk with them is worse than the fog; their look, even, is depressing. There are many varieties of such men. There is one variety which is peculiarly irritating, viz.: the conceited pessimist, the man who has an inordinately good opinion of himself, and who has somehow awakened to the fact that others (owing to their singular blindness and obtuseness) do not share it; he is a pessimist, because his hand is against every man. His uneasy conviction that he is not valued as he ought to be makes it certain to him that the times are out of joint. Then there is the pessimism of the disillusionized pleasure-seeker and of the whimpering sentimentalist; there is the pessimism of the dogmatist, who finds his own formulas are not universally accepted—the man who tells you that though there is much activity in religion, yet that men are weak in doctrine. Then there is the bitter cynicism of the newspaper satirist or of the magazine philosopher, and what is most piteous and pathetic of all, the silent bewilderment of those who cannot make it all out, who sit bewildered before the changed and changing order of the world with no hope for themselves or for others.

Many there be that survey the religious outlook, the social order, or the individual specimens of life around them, and cry, with no sign of expectation in their voices, 'Who will show us any good?'

And the strength of this utterance lies in the fact that it does not represent the most shallow view; it professes to look beneath the surface and to see through things, but it does not see far enough. The most superficial view of all is that of the cheerful optimist, who will not allow that there is anything amiss. Things have gone well with himself, and he is not disposed to allow that they can go wrong with anyone else.

The official ecclesiastical view about the Church of England generally adopts this attitude. No one would ever gather, from the rose-coloured descriptions of parishes and organizations which are often given, what are the gaps and leaks, what are the failures to touch and interest the real life of a parish.

The Church of England and her services have a great attraction for a certain class, and we are very thankful for the often excellent work she does among them; but there are whole regions of life in London which she only touches through the occasional accident of some gifted or sympathetic personality, not because those regions are incapable of being touched, but because she trusts too much to a machinery that has not been adapted to their wants and needs.

'Faith in machinery is our besetting sin,' says Matthew Arnold, 'often machinery absurdly disproportioned to the end, but always machinery as if it had a value in and for itself.' But the optimist who speaks in Convocation, or at a meeting of a Diocesan Conference, about the grand work which is being done, or who spouts his windy declamation at some packed meeting, has never looked at facts as they are; has only looked at the crowd in some popular church on a Sunday evening, and omitted to walk down some popular thoroughfare during church, and see there the crowd which neither the Church nor any other religious body touches.

No man then, either about religious or social life, can really look at things as they are and be contented with the sort of cheerful optimism which characterizes an Archdeacon's charge or a diocesan report. He goes deeper; he begins to look at things as they are, and then comes the day of danger; he is disillusioned, and he runs to the other extreme; because there are dull spots, there is no sun; because there are sick people, there is no health; because there are failures, there is no success. At this stage the man crawls like a rabbit into his hole, and seated there, he says, 'I have got through the surface and its simple presumptions; I have seen through things; *here* there is no sunlight, no beauty, all is dark and dreary and miserable; religion is played out.' He is below the surface; he has passed out of the stage of dreams and charms; he has seen many things, but has he got far enough yet? There is a further stage if a man gets deep enough, where he will learn to hope again—the stage where he sees not what things look like, but where he sees what life is for—that the object of life is not success nor failure, but to live for God and to live for man. Then, whether the sun shines or not; whether things are dark and dreary in religion, or whether he feels that its real power is telling; whether society is advancing or deteriorating, he is still able to hope, because he is trying to live for God and for man.

And then, further, the same voice, which taught him that, speaks to him about others also. He sees that untoward and crooked things mean education in character; that the experiences of life do not end in themselves, but that they have power to make men into something else; and so he passes into the centre—the middle of things. And then the lost things come back again; the failures that seemed to destroy everything come back as instruments of higher work—as the adjustment which is a necessity if he is ever to fill his God-appointed place. And thus hope begins to dawn.

'Experience,' says St. Paul, 'worketh hope.' How strange the saying sounds! And yet it does. The man who has gone through this experience has gained a deeper knowledge of God. He understands the drift of Christ's life better; he sees that, however hopeless things look, there is still Christ; there is still the Christ-appeal waiting, and scheming, and contriving to get itself heard by every man. He sees a living force within things—not a dead Christ, who has left a will which a cold and dogmatic priesthood, an autocratic ministry, are to interpret in set forms, and chilling sentences, and dignified warnings, but a living Christ, Whose heart is palpitating behind every unselfish action, and Who is living in every brave and noble endurance, and bearing Himself up under every failure, and spreading His Spirit wherever He can find a heart that will convey Him on and show Him to others.

He has made, then, the great discovery, not that everything is going on splendidly because religious machinery is so perfect, but the discovery that there is Christ in every unselfish movement of the day; that He is leading man to find Himself within man; that He is teaching men the deepest truths, that the Communion of Saints means that every life lives by every other life; that the Communion of His Sacred Body and Blood is not a reward for virtue or even only a means of individual growth, but a social symbol of man's communion with man, and that the unworthy communicant is he who does not find the Christ in others, Who is the Life of his life.

'The secret of vision,' says a great writer, 'is undying hope.' What we can hope for really, even two or three of us, of that we shall soon see the germs; what we do not hope for may be under our very feet, and we are blind, we cannot see it. Let us see what we can hope for, and then we shall get to what can we see—we who are yearning and longing to see it. We hope for a purer Church, a more Christ-like Church, than the world has ever seen—a Church whose creeds have become inspirations. We hope for the day when men will make 'God their religion, instead of making religion their God.' We hope for an ideal reunion, when men who are now with us in their wish to be with us, and in their wish to preserve the Christ-spirit of service, will be so one with us that we and they shall no longer talk of reunion, or get up misleading discussions to promote it, but shall find ourselves so enwrapped and so possessed by the Christ-spirit that we shall find division intolerable. Then, at last, we shall find a way of oneness with every heart that has translated into life the Christ command, 'As ye would that men should do unto you, even so do unto them;' we shall recognise that as the really encircling bond; we do so now in our deepest moments, but the conviction that it is so will grow and grow till God shows us the way to openly acknowledge it. We hope for the day when man will think of the service of man as the deepest religious privilege, when that ideal feet-washing shall somehow become practically expressed in all our lives; when men shall seek not for patronage, but for opportunities of service; when the Church shall be no more seen haggling for its rights, but anxious to let everyone see how every detail in the life of the community is dear to it, how it believes in trust and generous dealing, how it has caught the Christ-spirit of 'losing its life to save it.' We hope, too, to see the ideal of Christ's teaching in the State as in the Church. We hope to see men believing that He meant what He said; that the day of non-natural interpretation is over; that He intended to create a vast social change; to make the employer regard his workman as his brother; to make every man regard injury to woman as injury to his own sister; to lead men to find Himself not in some mystical dream, but in the often unselfconscious wants of those around them.

We hope, and we have grounds for hope; we are beginning to see the dawn of what fifty years ago would have been impossible. We have found that even companies can think of the bodies and souls of those whom they employ, as well as of their own dividends; we have found that it has at last dawned on all, in a measure, that man is more than money, character than possessions, purity and decency than high rents. To the young we appeal, to those who will carry these beginnings on by God's help to brighter conclusions than we shall live to see. To them we would say, 'Be true to facts as they are, study them, acknowledge them; be afraid of the cant and dishonesty that bolsters up anything merely because it is our own; but at the same time learn to recognise beneath the most untoward and unpromising things the workings of Christ; see them in what seems to be the unavailing protest; see them in the growing shame of acknowledged selfishness; see them in the more righteous public utterances of our leading statesmen; see them in the spirit that sets on foot everywhere new means for benefiting the social life of people—in clubs, in polytechnics, and in all agencies of the kind. Above all, believe in the power of human aspiration when touched by the living Christ. Hope everything from man because of the Divine possibilities within him. And when he disappoints you, and when you find no appreciation and no response, still remember your place is among your brethren, however far they may stray.' We have a sure ally in everyone through the Divinely-planted instinct of human aspiration. Above all, we have the certainty that Christ is at work with others as with ourselves; that God has a voice through Christ for every one of His children, and that in a thousand ways of which we never know, if we catch the real social spirit of Christ, even we may help to translate that voice to them.

THE SOCIAL OUTLOOK.

BY THE

REV. PROFESSOR H. C. SHUTTLEWORTH,
RECTOR OF ST. NICHOLAS, COLE ABBEY.

'*I am not come to destroy, but to fulfil.*'—ST. MATTHEW v. 17.

OUR LORD spoke these words, standing between two worlds; the old world which was passing, the new world which began with Him. He is expounding the old law in its relation to the new order, and in these words He gives us the principle of true progress. The world has advanced and grown, and must always advance and grow, not by destruction, but by fulfilment. Old institutions, old laws, old ideas, cease to be effective, and pass away or are driven out; but out of them, and from what they have accomplished, is born the new world. The future is the child of the past.

And we, to-day, as this eventful century draws near its close, stand at the meeting-point of an old world and a new. Dean Stanley, in his funeral sermon on Lord Palmerston, told his hearers that with the death of that Minister a new order had begun; that they stood 'on the watershed of the dividing streams.' That saying would be far more true of our own day; not only because we recognise the close of an epoch in the retirement of the last, greatest, and best of the long line of our commercial statesmen. Everywhere, old ways of thinking are being superseded, old institutions are sharply criticised, old moralities questioned. New ideas are in the air, our politics and our social order are being transformed, our national life seems to be taking another direction. Naturally, there are some among us who look upon the change with suspicion and dislike, and fear for its not distant consequences. It is not to be wondered at. Old institutions are venerable and picturesque; they have done good work in their day, and perhaps may yet do more. Old customs and ideas are tenderly associated with our own best memories, with our recollections of former years, and of the dear dead who made those years bright for us. And thus the fading out of the old world seems like the death of a dear friend, or the pulling down of the old house where we spent our childhood. Christ looked with kindly tolerance upon those who thus clung to the old order. ' *No man having drunk old wine straightway desireth new; for he saith, the old is better.*' Yet from among them there spring prophets of mourning, and lamentation, and woe, whose burden is one of despair and gloom, with no note of hope or gleam of faith. About a year ago we were all reading a 'Forecast' of this depressing sort, by an able and cultivated pessimist, who has no enthusiasm for the new ideas, and who looks forward to the coming in of the newer order with calm, sad resignation. A brighter and, we may believe, a truer view of 'social evolution' has just come into our hands, which might almost be described as an exposition in terms of history of the text I have chosen for to-day. The *laudator temporis acti* must be tenderly dealt with, the pessimist must be answered, by those of us who believe that the twentieth century will be a day of fuller life and richer hope than the ages which have gone before it.

It is equally natural that, on the other hand, an epoch of transition like the present should produce abnormal and irregular growths, strange types, which are neither of the old nor of the new. There are men who think that the best means of heralding the new dawn is to fling a bomb into a crowd of harmless people. There are those who believe, with Bakunin, that the only way to regenerate society is to wipe it out by utter destruction, in the belief that a new and better order will surely be evolved out of chaos. It never has been so, and it never can be so. Such methods can only delay the advance of progress. You can, indeed, cast out devils by Beelzebub. But you cannot keep them out; only angels can do that. 'His kingdom shall not stand': for by fulfilment, not by destruction, the old passes into the new.

As we endeavour to make our social outlook to-day, it seems as though there is but one other period in the history of the modern world which compares with our own time; one other such a breaking up of the fountains of the great deep, such submerging of ancient landmarks in the flood of new ways and new thoughts. That former crisis came when the Roman Empire went down before the irresistible onrush of the northern tribes. In that *débacle*, it seemed certain that all which the older world had won, of knowledge, of civilization, of law, would be overwhelmed and swept to fragments by the flood of conquering barbarism. It was saved by one institution: the Christian Church. Such is the common consent of all historians, from Gibbon to Guizot, from Sismondi to Sir James Stephen. Out of that hideous confusion of blood and destruction, the Church created modern Europe. Against physical force she opposed spiritual ideals; she made it possible for the old order to grow into the new. The Church was the mediator, her bishops true *pontifices*—builders of bridges across the gulf which threatened to swallow up 'the old perfections of the world.'

And now modern Europe is itself passing away, to give place to a new age and a new order of things. Not now, as of old, is it a horde of barbarians which sweeps down upon fair lands and beautiful cities, to be won and held by force of arms. But men and women are now claiming their part in the good things of life; they are marching upon the privileges and the possessions which the few have hitherto held, and demanding their rightful share. Revolutions, we know, are not made with rose-water; and when 'the brute despair of trampled centuries' finds a voice and gropes for its rights, there is likely enough to be a good deal of wild talk uttered, and, it may be, wild work done.*

Is there a place for the saviour of the old world among the forces which are re-making society to-day? Once, her bitterest foes being her judges, the Church saved civilization and humanized the conquerors. Alone among the institutions of Western Europe which passed through that former catastrophe, the Church is still here. Can she do for us to-day what she did for the world long ago?

What are the invading forces, and what is their battle-cry?

1. The first is the great army of Labour. All over the civilized world, the workman has arrived. He is possessing himself of political power, and he is resolved to use it to the full. He has been marvellously patient through centuries of oppression and exploitation; and his patience is coming to an end. Patience is not always a virtue, and contentment is sometimes a crime; and however we may wonder at and admire the astonishing patience of the poor, we must admit that the atmosphere of content does not breed reformers. The labourer is claiming his right. He has not received, and he does not receive, he tells us, the due reward of his toil. He demands a share—a rightful share—of the wealth he helps so largely to create. He wants a more decent house to live in, a better wage, less exhausting hours of work, more leisure, more certainty of employment. He has surely a just ground of complaint against a society which dooms him to face depression and want every few years, and condemns him in old age to the workhouse. And his claim is made in the sacred name of Justice. He marches under the banner of his Right.

No Christian can treat lightly such a plea. It is signifi-

* W. T. Stead, 'Vatican Letters,' pp. 28, 29.

cant that the workman's case is founded upon a moral, not a utilitarian, basis. He does not ask whether it would pay to grant his demands; he only asks whether it is not right and just that he should enjoy the fruit of his labour.

My friends, we are bound to face this fact, that while labour thus appeals to morals we are often apt to decline the appeal, and merely to ask whether changes will pay, especially whether they will pay ourselves. Is that worthy of those who profess to take Christ for their Master? We may, if we please, proceed to make inquiry into the justice of labour's claim. But unless we are prepared to accept the appeal to Right and Justice, and at the least to examine it, we are deliberately taking a lower standard than the workman. The Church is pledged by the very charter of her existence to accept his principles, and to proceed to inquire whether indeed they justify his conclusion. If what he asks is indeed just and right, it must be granted, cost what it may.

It may reasonably be feared that at a time when so much stress is laid upon the bettering of material conditions, there may be a danger of forgetting spiritual ideals. Man cannot live without bread, yet he does not live by bread alone. It is right that every man should have equal opportunity; yet the life is more than meat. Possibly it may be the work of the Christian Church, in this time of transition, to preserve and maintain the spiritual basis upon which all material improvement must be founded, if, indeed, it is to endure. In this she can command the co-operation of the English labour leaders. It is noteworthy that nearly all of them are religious men, earnest Christians, who place things spiritual in the forefront of their work. 'The labour movement,' said one of these men in my hearing, 'is a religious movement above all.'

Can the Church do other than help, and bless, and guide? Her Founder was a workman, His Apostles were labourers. Her glory is that she has ever been the Church of the poor. Time was, in our own England, when it was to the Church that the workman looked for consolation and protection and help. How is it that to-day the workman suspects the Church of his nation, and too often regards her as the strongest and the bitterest of the foes arrayed against him? O you of the City of London! the centre and heart of English commerce and English social life! how far is this your fault? How far is it due to our habitual appeal to utilitarianism rather than to justice, to our preference of the trader's question, 'Will it pay?' to the workman's question, 'Is it right?'

Upon the answer depends the decision of our former question, Whether or no the Church can do to-day what she did for the older world?

2. There is another invading army, whose onward march is perhaps more significant, more pregnant with consequences to the future of the race, than even the approach of the hosts of Labour. What is roughly called the Woman question is by far the most momentous of our time. In the English-speaking countries, at least, the women are claiming a new position, and are beginning to advance towards its attainment. Woman, like Labour, is demanding what she regards as a right, a long-delayed measure of justice. She, too, asks for a career, for liberty to live her own life, to do her own work, to take her share in the government and local administration of her country. The first positions are already carried; the principle is practically admitted as just. Inevitably, here also, the time of transition has brought forth strange and unnatural products. The 'Wild Women' of a certain gifted, if somewhat unbalanced, woman-writer are not altogether creatures of the imagination. The mistake is to look upon Dodo and her kind as true representatives of the coming woman. They are, in truth, representatives of the middle period, between the old and the new; they are types, and accurate types, of life in a time of unrest and change such as this.

What has the Christian Church to say to the claims, the pleas, the demands of Woman for her rightful place in the new world? There are certain sanctities which the Church must guard and preserve, in the highest and most necessary interests of the race. There are principles which she has received from her Lord as the most holy of trusts. There are fundamental moralities with which the Church can brook no paltering. She dare not look lightly upon the loosening of the marriage bond. She cannot forget that no nation has ever lasted long which has admitted any possible basis of society other than that of nature—the family. But outside the sanctuary of these most holy things, the Church can have nothing but encouragement and help for those who claim their due, in the name of Justice. The Church, which enthrones the Madonna, and daily sings her hymn; the Church, which emancipated Woman from the degrading chattel-servitude of an older time; the Church, which first gave woman a career, in her religious houses and her philanthropic institutions; the Church, which has ever been the protector and the helper of the oppressed; the Church cannot choose but bid Godspeed to woman's new crusade, which does but carry to a conclusion the onward movement that the Church herself began. Here, as elsewhere, 'the Christ that is to be' comes, not to destroy, but to fulfil.

It is He that sitteth upon the throne who ever maketh all things new. If the foundations of things are shaken, who is it that shaketh the heavens and the earth? Times of transition are times of confusion and perplexity, but they are times of hope and faith. For in the passing of the old world, and the incoming of the new, we find a new revelation of the Christ who works in history, and makes Himself more plain before the face of man, as the ages sweep onward to their destined goal.

When the church of the Eternal Wisdom at Constantinople was captured by the hosts of Islam, and turned into a mosque, the great mosaic figure of the Christ enthroned in glory over the east was defaced and blotted out with paint. But as the years went by, the imperishable mosaic wore its way, so to say, through the fading veil, and the calm Face once more looked down upon those who bowed beneath. Some day, of a surety, that veil shall be removed, and the throned and glorified figure of the Christ shall glow in more than its ancient splendour above adoring Christian crowds.

Even so has the face and figure of Jesus, the Son of God, been dimmed by the folly and selfishness of His own disciples, by the greed and cruelty and sloth of men. Still He looks upon us with inspiring and humbling gaze; still His hand is uplifted in perpetual blessing. More and more clearly, as His creation moves towards that far-off Divine event, we seem to see Him; and when the smoke and dust of change has cleared away, lo, the Divine face is yet more plain to our eyes. For the evolution of man and of the world is but the clearer and completer manifestation of the Christ.

THE END.

Elliot Stock, 62, Paternoster Row, London, E.C.

www.ingramcontent.com/pod-product-compliance
Lightning Source LLC
Chambersburg PA
CBHW031820230426
43669CB00009B/1208